Stop Thinking Like That

No Matter What

Jason Hyland

To James,
You're never alone
There's always hope.
Keep up the Great work.

conceive. believe
achieve-
★always★

ISBN-13: 978-1984383518

Printed in the United States of America

www.jason-hyland.com

Cover Design: Achraf Lahmame, @achraflahmame

Follow the author: @Jasonrhyland

[Dedication]

To all those sick and suffering, may you find the help you deserve.

[Preface]

Stop Thinking Like That is book of action! Indispensable knowledge for creating a better life is now at your fingertips. This is a book for anyone that wants to live a happier life. It is for anyone who is facing challenges that have brought them to the bottom. It is not only for alcoholics and addicts, *Stop Thinking Like That* is for EVERYONE out there because no one is exempt from facing hardship. I want to help you find out who the best you is. I want you to wake up with a smile every morning. I want to fill your mind with positivity. I want to leave you hungry for greatness. I want you to experience the best life possible.

Writing *Stop Thinking Like That* is not for any of the recognition that may come with it. I am writing to help others find themselves, which in turn helps me become a better person. This book is about the journey we all take in life through the ups and downs, the tears and the smiles, and our response to each situation. It is about building ourselves up to being the best possible person we can be. It is about stepping into the unknown, out of our comfort zone and into the uncomfortable, to find out who we really are. It is for the men and women who are isolated inside their homes scared to show their face to the world because of the things they *had* done. It is about facing our past and challenging the adversity that comes with it head on. The stories I will be sharing with you throughout *Stop Thinking Like That* symbolize that ANYTHING is possible in life.

There are no odds too great for us to overcome. Life is beautiful, so please do me a favor and SMILE!

Are you living in isolation hopeless that you'll never be able to overcome your addiction? Stop Thinking Like That. Is your heart broken due to a tough breakup or bitter divorce and you fear you're not worthy enough to find love again? Stop Thinking Like That. Did you just get fired from your dream job and feel as if you are destined for a life struggling financially living paycheck to paycheck? Stop Thinking Like That. Have you accepted that you will never get in the shape you desire, forever feeling unhealthy? Stop Thinking Like That.

Today is the day to stop thinking like you will not succeed in life and to stop thinking that you will not find happiness. No longer will you be held back by this false pretense of disbelief. Today you will succeed. Today you will smile at yourself in the mirror. Today you will love and be loved. Today you will find joy in your relationships. Today you will be happy! Now, go ahead and enjoy!

[Acknowledgements]

This amazing journey that I am traveling on certainly hasn't been a solo mission. Without the support, forgiveness, and unconditional love from my mother Jill and step-father Paul, none of this would have ever been possible. You are the parents that make dreams come true. Thank you, Mum, for always reminding me that I can do anything if I put my mind to it. There will never be enough words to show my gratitude for having you as my mother. And to Paul, thank you for not giving up on me. You inspire me every single day and have shown me what it takes to be a real man in every aspect of life. I love you both, to bits.

My journey began in the Danvers detox facility where I walked in as a completely broken individual. During my month long stay there I regained my self-worth, self-esteem, and my confidence, which were the driving forces behind getting better every day while helping others at the same time. This was due to the amazing staff upstairs, from admissions to counselors, and all the RS's. Thank you all for saving my life. You'll always hold a special place in my heart.

Moving into the Link House in Newburyport is where the real work began as I was now living back out in society, but with *some* restrictions. From day one, I received the support and discipline necessary to help me grow as an individual, while regaining a sense of structure and taking on the responsibilities needed to live a life full of happiness, joy, and success.

To my counselor Kerry, thank you for putting up with me during my best and worst of times. Dealing with all my bitching and complaining couldn't have been easy, but you continued to demand more out of me, pushing me to be better every day No Matter What. You knew I held more potential within and unleashed me to find it. Thank you for believing in me and my passion, never once discouraging me from my vision. Heidi, you are amazing at what you do. Your constant positive energy radiated throughout the entire house. Your soothing words personally helped me heal and your support in my endeavors kept me moving forward. Vicky, you'll never get rid of me and for good reason. Thanks for keeping me sane. Bob, I owe you all the credit for getting me in there, thank you. And to Linda, thank you for allowing me to visit my 'girlfriend' every day at the library. It worked. I'll be forever grateful for my six months in the house.

To all the men who became friends and brothers during my stay at the Link; do not EVER lose hope and always remember you are not alone. Love you guys. Dare to be great!

Our paths in recovery show us who are real friends are. There are three that never left my side since grade school. Gus, I cannot thank you enough for being the best friend I could possibly ask for. Since meeting on an all-star team back in our little leagues days through the hardest of times battling my inner demons and onto my new beginnings in recovery, you have always been there for me. Ty, even from across the pond you took time out of chasing your own personal dreams and were always there to talk. You never stopped believing in me and your constant encouragement kept me going through all the adversity of the everyday struggles of early recovery. Finally, to Matt. Even though we only see each other roughly once every five years, we are brothers from another mother. I will always have your back and I know you mine, as we battle through this one day at a time. I love you all for sticking by my side without blinking an eye. Thank you.

To all of the great people I've met in Newburyport, thank you. Your community was beyond welcoming amidst the constant turnover you witness at the house. The overwhelming support gives the Link House men the hope and strength to uplift us during very trying times. The altruistic ways of the community are simply a blessing. A special thanks to the men and women who personally helped me and shall remain anonymous. And to the members of the ICC and Congregational Church who so graciously took time out of their lives to service us, as well as the less fortunate in the community, I thank you from the bottom of my heart. You showed me the true meaning of compassion.

To the staff of the Newburyport Public Library, I appreciate your patience, kindliness, and willingness to help out whenever needed while I wrote *Stop Thinking Like That* on one of your public computers.

To my Hyland family, Scott, Jennifer, and Nana. I love you all dearly and I thank you for your patience with this process. Dad, I know you are looking down and guiding me each day, so I do not end up where you did from this disease. Rest easy.

And to all the other individuals who have had a part in the making of *Stop Thinking Like That;* childhood friend and serial entrepreneur Mike Beatrice, fantastic author also in recovery Sarah Ordo, and entrepreneur Lindsey Cartwright. Thank you all for taking the time out of your busy lives to assist in helping make my vision a reality. To bestselling author and entrepreneur Mike Alden. Thank you for helping me muster up the courage to *ask more* to *get more* out of life.

And finally, to all those before me who have inspired by their enviable knowledge for creating a better life for ourselves, thank you for pioneering the way. Every day I read and listen to your words, constantly pushing me to strive to be the best possible me there is. Too many to name, but know if you have an inspirational or motivational You-Tube video out there and or a book promoting self-betterment, your works work!

My journey in life has just begun and I am beyond excited to see what the future has in store for me. As long as I take it one day at a time anything is possible. I know great things await because I BELIEVE. I am extremely grateful knowing I have all of y'all alongside me on this path to greatness. Thank you everyone!

To Beanie and Shaq, Daddy's home!!!

[Contents]

[Introduction]

"Folks are usually about as happy as they make up their minds to be."

- Abraham Lincoln -

First and foremost, let me say thank you. Thank you for giving a chance to this lost, hopeless, low-down alcoholic. Thank you for helping me reach out toward my dreams. I will be forever grateful for you and it is my intention that you will be saying those exact words back to me by the end of this journey together.

For far too many years my life was a fragile existence completely managed by my obsession for always wanting *more*. Whether it be alcohol, drugs, sex, money, work, or working out, I needed as much as I could get my hands on and I needed it instantly. I became addicted to anything and everything that I believed would give me that high feeling of briefly numbing reality for me. I had managed to lose everything that ever mattered to me along this path of destruction. My life had become so unmanageable and completely hopeless that my poor mother was told to start preparing for my funeral as her only child was inevitably going to succumb to this disease.

I was on the verge of achieving my lifelong dream of playing Major League Baseball after my sophomore year of college that culminated in my receiving of the College World Series MVP. Not even six months later I was searching for a new school to take me in because my obsessions got me kicked off the team I had just helped to the National Championship game. The loss of my true love in life, baseball, was the beginning of the end for me as my addictions began to overtake my world.

This book is by no means about all my drunken escapades, although I could certainly write an entire novel on that subject alone. But it is about the courage, fortitude, vulnerability, desire, and determination, absolutely whatever was needed to pick myself up off hell's dirty rotten floor and begin to transform my life, one day at a time. The over-sized ego that had led me to the depths of a desolate abyss I never knew existed had to be checked at the door and I suggest you do the same. Mixing in substances to an already depressed, hopeless, broken individual only further fueled the fire. I was completely lost in life, with my dream derailed, my family avoiding me at all costs, debt up to my eyeballs, and a credit score tanking worse than the New York Jets so I chose to isolate into a deep self-induced coma of despair.

Everything changed on a July morning during the summer of '17. I woke up and something was inexplicably different. I wasn't in a panic about how I was going to get my next fix, that I had no alcohol leftover, or that a negative symbol was attached to my bank account, but instead I felt a sense of complete calmness come over me. I wish there were better words to describe this feeling, but all I can say is that divine intervention was taking place and I wholeheartedly knew that day would be the end of the nightmare. The following morning, I began what would be the first day of the rest of my life.

My road to recovery has led me right into your hands (or headphones for you audiobookers) and I could not be happier. I am blessed to be included on your personal voyage to finding the best possible version of you that is inside just waiting to burst out. We are going to laugh and cry along the way, battling our inner demons together, and forever defeating the fear that has been holding us back from achieving true happiness. We will dig deep into our failures, our past defeats, no matter how bad it hurts, to learn from those experiences so we will know triumph moving forward. Put your big boy/girl pants on because there is going to be some tough love along the way. But in the end, amidst all the blood, sweat, and tears you will see that your life is full of so much promise and it is yours for the taking. Now raise up that Lombardi Trophy and scream at the top of your lungs "Let's Go!" like you are Tom F*cking Brady. But seriously, let's go!

Before we get started, I need to enlighten you with this...

I know you miss me, buddy. This is the longest we have *ever* been apart. The first week or so was terrible without you. I kept waking up sweating bullets and trembling in fear that this might really be the end to our decade long courtship. We started out like any other friendship, getting together during the weekends or on special occasions. We had some really great times together that is for sure. Breaking rules and hearts, running from the law, hitting triple digits on the freeway, and endless laughs at our rebellious life we lived together. I certainly will never forget our times as one, I promise you that.

Soon our weekend ventures turned into week night rendezvous'. Tuesday nights were dart nights, and, well, you cannot play darts by yourself, so I brought you along. And then we started hanging out every Thursday night so we could kick off our weekends early. We were slowly becoming BFFs; you really just made my life better. You were my one friend who was always there for me, who never argued with me, and who made me feel completely comfortable accepting the life we had built together.

It seemed like every girlfriend I had was very jealous of all our time we spent together. The countless nights listening to them cry angry tears and trying to keep you and me apart had little effect on our ever-building relationship. Girlfriends come and go, but I knew you and I had a very special bond that was destined to last forever and I was NOT going to let any girl get in the way of that

Remember when you moved in with me for good? Ah, the glory days when nothing else mattered. I even started to bring you to work with me every morning. I couldn't just let you sleep in all day and then have to wait until dinner time to see each other. My co-workers must have thought I had a real weak bladder with the amount of times they assuredly saw me up and leave the office. Little did they know I was secretly hanging out with you in OUR Jeep listening to sports talk radio? And yes, I call it *our* jeep because I would never go for a drive without you right by my side. We were truly becoming inseparable.

Doctors eventually tried their best to intervene, taking me away from you for days on end. Not once, not twice, not three times, but seven times total in one year alone. Like I told everyone else, "Sorry doc, but he is my best friend and I cannot live without him." They shook their heads in disbelief, knowing how unhealthy our relationship was fearing it could turn deadly. When they finally let me go home, I immediately ran right to you and we would be back to our ways together.

And how I could I forget my mother's feelings about our unbreakable bond? She treated it like a high school relationship, like it was just some obsession. She simply was unaware of how strong our bond together was. I thought she was just doing the motherly thing and did not want to see her only child get hurt. So, I told her you moved out and that we only hung out on occasion. But then when I would show up to see her she immediately knew I was still spending time with you and gave me a look of disgust. Again, I felt like she was just doing what any mother would if they feared for their child's safety. She even collaborated with the doctors and nurses and they all ganged up on me at once. I could see the gravity of the moment by the expressions on their faces, a look of desperation. I still did not understand, though, what the problem was with our growing friendship? You filled me up inside when I was empty, something neither they nor anyone else could do. So finally, everyone left us alone, and we had freedom at last. The phone calls ceased. No more texts. As long as I was with you there was no more seeing any of them.

You remember when you had finally taken my father's life after a four-plus decade relationship? Our bond was too tight for that to happen so I knew you would never do that to me and we became closer than ever, spending every second with you right by my side, no matter the time of day. No more girlfriend to bother us, no more work to go to, and no more family to deal with. Everyone was completely hopeless that we were going to BFF's until the end. Their constant reminders of what my dad's best friend did to him and other friends slowly faded away. They all finally accepted our friendship as it was; indestructible. Nothing else mattered to me anymore as long as I had you.

Life went on without incident and the days turned into months. We had our routine and we were sticking to it. Right when I woke up I had to immediately find you. I couldn't start my day without you. We locked all the doors, pulled down all the curtains, and threw away every responsibility in life so we could go on forever together.

After a few months of monotony, I realized you were becoming an expensive friend to keep around for breakfast, lunch, and dinner. But no person could ever get in between us so I certainly wasn't going to let money get in our way. I knew I had to have you by my side at all times so I did whatever it took to assure our time together would never end. I would take you with me at night and we scoured neighborhood after neighborhood in search of your empty friends. Once we filled up the back of our jeep we knew we'd have another day together. And we would repeat this day after day. But I was getting tired of this degrading process draining me. So, I had a solution. I knew my family would never help us stay together, and I came up with a plan to get them back and allow us to stay glued together. I found money, lots of it, and I took it when no one was looking. The plan was working remarkably!

With each passing day, though, your company was filling my insides less and less. And did you see what you had done to me physically? I didn't take you in and let you stay with me every single day for the past five years only to have you make me feel worse about myself. You never told me about the belly you were going to give me. You never said anything about it being harder to breathe the more we hung out. That it would affect simple things like walking up the stairs and doing dishes. You just laughed at me and even turned the shower off on me for days on end. But I still couldn't let you go. We had been together for far too long to give up now, so I pushed on. The bills continued to pile up, the loneliness become a daily thing, the same clothes entrenched my body day after day, my teeth were becoming more and more rotten, and even my dogs bellies began to get bigger. What did they ever do to you that you wouldn't even allow me to walk them?

If I tried to even cut back a little time with you, you would make me feel even worse, inside and out. You had completely taken over my life holding all the power. Every single thing I did was for you. And now the same people who I cut off for you wanted to talk to me all of a sudden. Their pile of money just didn't look right. It had dwindled down to the bottom, and I soon followed. You had won. Game over.

But then something miraculous occurred. Of all the things you had taken from me over the years and all the strength you possessed, you forgot about one thing. I am a child of God and He had finally broken through the never-ending pile of shit we had built together called my life. His words were simple, yet more powerful than anything you could ever do to me. I went to sleep that night knowing that I would finally say good bye to you forever when I woke up.

So, the next day, before saying our final goodbyes, I did something I was not able to do in many, many years. I told my family the truth. There were no more lies. Every single tear that I had been holding in because I feared your wrath poured down my cheeks. I finally felt free. Then, another miracle occurred. My family accepted me and wanted to help me. The same family that seemed to have drifted away, like Wilson did to Hanks, but fortunately for me my raft caught up to them in the nick of time. They realized the power you possessed over me was far greater than all of ours combined. They realized you controlled my entire life. They realized everything I did was for you. And they knew that your plan all along was to take my life. And they knew, I alone, could not stop you from achieving your goal.

I packed you up into *my* jeep and off we went. You knew something was up when I took you down to the beach, solo. We had many great times down there during our time together, but all of that was about to finally be put in the rearview, for good. After we had one last moment together I did one more thing that I hadn't done in many, many years, something I had never been able to do since the day we first met nearly twenty years ago. I finally freed myself from your no longer impeccable grasp and watched the ocean waves take you away. Forever

[1]

Life is Good Today

"To get something you never had you have to do something you've never did."

- Nelson Mandela -

I'm dancing away as I walk through the center of campus past the central waterfall feature oblivious to anyone around me. Confident? Check! Happy? Check! Grateful? Check! I mean, you must feel good about life if you're doing the Macarena amidst a mass of students rushing in between classes. Yeah baby, I got my Mojo back! (insert Austin Powers voice!)

Soon I realize the scene playing out before my eyes is nothing but a dream. It's 6:01am and the radio alarm clock's playing the groovy tune I was just breaking down to on my college campus in Tampa. Talk about a wakeup call! How could I not be feeling good about getting my day started? Not too long ago I was waking up every few hours drenched in sweat, shaking, and wondering what I did so wrong that God had to take away my ability to dream. Hadn't he taken enough away already? My girl has moved out. My employer has fired me. My family has abandoned me. My bank account is in the red. My Jeep has an empty tank. As if it couldn't get any worse everyone then seems to want something from me, the poor guy with absolutely nothing. One collection agency wants this much. Another agency wants that much. The TV and phone companies threaten to shut off their services if I don't give them this amount. The vet needs to see my dogs for their shots AND they want me to pay them for it. The audacity! Don't all these damn people realize I have priorities and sitting alone on the top, high above everything else is Jason's needs? Not theirs!

I turn the radio up a bit more and listen to the remainder of the song. Once I finish writing out my gratitude list I ask my God (Higher Power, Buddha, whatever you may choose to believe in) for guidance throughout the day ahead. I tell myself "Today's going to be a great day!", then rise to my feet, and finish by making my bed. The simple task of making our bed each morning is a positive trait we can carry into our day ahead. My pillow is as dry as the Sahara and the only shaking my body is doing is due to the beats the alarm clock was spitting out. And no headache, to boot! My arms rise high behind me as I arch far back, stretching, and let out a big *ahhh* like a lion roaring as he awakes from his slumber. Hakuna Matatta indeed!

The positive energy flowing throughout my entire body each morning upon waking up is a far cry from the soulless being who awoke searching for remnants of alcohol or drugs he might have forgot about the prior night. I wake up with a feeling of purpose, something that had escaped me for the last decade of my life. I can honestly say I wake up excited for the day ahead, confident that I will end it clean, sober, and with peace of mind that had long evaded me. Alcohol and drugs destroyed my mind, body, and soul for longer than I am proud to say. But, with each passing day, the little sliver of hope that I found back on that sunny July day, grows more and more. That sliver is gaining momentum, fast, and I could not be more excited for what the future holds for me.

"I'm chasing dreams, but never sleep."

- Mackelmore *Glorious* -

A lot of people I have met throughout my recovery process like to ask me "How?". How am I, in the early stages of recovery, full of such positivity, happiness, and confidence? How am I not in a deep depression, constantly shedding tears about all the damage my past has caused? How am I anything close to confident that it is all over? How can I speak with enthusiasm and vigor, and with such strong conviction that the nightmare is finally behind me? Don't get me wrong, these are very valid questions. And I will answer them for you, but I need you to BELIEVE. Have FAITH in what I am about to tell you. Because if you do not then you will struggle to find the peace that you deserve and the joy that can fill your life.

Let's start at the beginning of every morning when my eyes open up to a fresh new day. Once I'm up I immediately begin to collect the moments from the dreams I was just having. Yes, dreams. You see, dreams did not exist during the height of my addiction to alcohol and drugs. They were that mythical creature, the unicorn that you always heard of, but could never seem to find. I was endlessly searching for the non-existent. Reminiscing about my dreams is now the first part of each day for me. I know how precious dreams are because I had them taken away from me for so long. And you know what they say, "You don't know what you've got 'til it's gone"? Well, that is as true a statement that exists when it comes to dreams.

The entire time I was stuck battling the bottle or drug coinciding with the depression I was living in a never-ending nightmare. A nightmare is defined as an unpleasant dream, and for my life that definition is a complete understatement. And unfortunately for me, my nightmare was not just an unpleasant dream, it was reality. This is why today I cherish any dream I may have, the good and the bad.

The devil still likes to show his repulsive face on many an occasion during my sleep. But, he controls me no longer. I now resist the devil by deciding to turn my will and my life over to my Higher Power whom I choose to call God.

One of the most influential men in this world for many an addict is MLB all-star Josh Hamilton. In his book *Beyond Belief* he states how he consistently said out loud to himself the following Bible verse daily to help him get over any temptations that may arise during his recovery; "Humble yourself before God. Resist the devil and he will flee." James 4:7-8. And that is exactly what I do. Every single day. I no longer live in that unpleasant dream anymore, but instead I start my day thinking about all the dreams that used to elude me.

The story of Josh Hamilton was a well-publicized journey of one man's life battling his addiction to drugs and alcohol. More so, it is as powerful of an example you will find in overcoming the odds when all the chips are stacked against you. Josh has always been a true inspiration for me personally because I could relate to him more than I could anyone I formally knew. I might not have been the #1 pick in the MLB draft, nor had half as much talent as he did, but I certainly did have enough talent to fulfill my dream of playing for a Major League Baseball organization and it was derailed due to my addictions.

Josh finally had his disease in a vice-grip when he found himself standing center stage in one of the most famous cathedrals in all of sports, Yankee Stadium (it isn't Fenway Park, but it is remarkable nonetheless). The whole world had their eyes on greatness as he stood in the batter's box during that Home Run Derby. His athletic abilities speak for themselves, but the greatness I witnessed that evening was his perseverance, determination, and whatever-it-takes attitude that so many of us cannot find the courage to seek out.

I had the honor to meet Josh in 2012 when my beloved Red Sox were hosting his Texas Rangers. My inside's shook greatly as I spoke with him briefly after the game outside of the visitor's locker-room, handing him a Project Purple band that I received a few weeks earlier from another major source of inspiration in Chris Herren (we'll get more into his story in the pages to come). The following Sunday night on ESPN's nationally televised game Josh was wearing that band as his team played in front of millions. Yes, Josh has had his battles with the disease in the years since and will forever battle the demons of addiction, but he proved to me and thousands of others that anything is possible if we believe in ourselves and are willing to put in the work. I will always be much appreciative and grateful for the hope that Josh brought to me during those tough years of my life.

Today my days are off to fantastic starts before they even begin. When I am awoken from these dreams I immediately remember that I am safe and healthy, eager to get my day going. I cannot ask for a much better start to my day than that. The feeling I have upon waking up today is completely indescribable in comparison to how I felt just a few short months ago.

For the alcoholics and addicts reading this, I know how you feel when you wake up. I know you probably are tossing and turning throughout the entire night, lucky to get an hour or two of actual sleep. I know there is a good possibility you are waking up in a puddle of sweat, trembling, and feeling downright shitty. Your stomach is most likely flipping around like a gold medal gymnast. I am sure you begin to search for any booze you may have misplaced or simply forgot about from the night prior. You look for your cell phone to text your dealers, hoping it has enough juice because you undoubtedly forgot to put it on the charger before you *passed* out. The thought of withdrawal has now taken over your mind and will NOT leave until you satiate that feeling. Withdrawal may very well be the single most unpleasant feeling that exists. It truly is a living hell. The list of things that I am grateful for could fill this entire book and a withdrawal free day is perched damn near the top.

These days, once I am up and out of bed, I get right down on my knees to have a conversation with my Higher Power. I talk with Him like I do anyone else I speak to during my day. I ask Him to look over me throughout the day and help me spread the message of hope and inspiration to the best of my ability to those in need. Helping others helps me stay humble, grateful, and sober. I finish with a prayer, thank Him, and am then ready to dominate the day ahead.

"If God is for us, who can be against us?"

-Romans 8:31-

Here comes a crazy thought. Next, I go into the bathroom and...wait for it...brush my teeth! The same teeth I so terribly abused with copious amounts of sugary booze, letting rot for days on end without seeing a toothbrush, are now receiving the TLC they deserve. You'll read later about what my poor teeth have gone through since my childhood; I hope you have an empty stomach.

Our addictions utterly destroy our bodies, whether it be from alcohol, drugs, food, sex, sleep or lack thereof, and so forth. The least we can do is wash ourselves, brush our teeth, and mix in a shave every now and then. But no! The true alcoholic, the true addict, the true loser says *fuck it* and lets his or her appearance fall by the waaayyy side to the point that their family and friends no longer recognize them. One day you are the prom queen the next you are looking like Lindsey Lohan after a bender in Vegas. We begin to "forget" to brush our teeth and avoid showering like it's the plague because it takes too much effort. I didn't shave for months on end letting my overgrown beard cover up my fat, bloated face. And you know what the sad thing is? We do not even give a shit! Soon we also do not recognize the person in the mirror (if we can even stomach looking in mirrors anymore).

Showering today never felt so good. Go try it out, I promise it won't hurt. And maybe you won't smell like the dumpster behind McDonald's anymore. Maybe people won't move a few seats over when you walk onto the city bus because of the stench eroding from your body? Getting back into the habit of brushing my teeth and showering daily were a BIG step in learning to love myself again. If we cannot take care of ourselves how can we possibly take care of our children, loved ones, pets, and others? If we cannot love ourselves, how in the world can we love anyone else? A refreshing shower and thorough brushing of your teeth may just be the kick start you need to get your life back on track. It is the simple things, TRUST me.

Once showered up, you are fresh 'n clean and ready to dominate the day ahead! Walk out that front door confident, proud, and full of the positive energy that we spoke of earlier. Our mind is the most powerful thing that has ever been created. It can do wondrous things for us if we truly want it to. The late great Napoleon Hill, author of one of the most influential books I have ever read, *Think and Grow Rich* puts it best; "What the mind can conceive, and believe, the mind can achieve!" This is something that I have practiced since the first day I read it nearly a decade ago and the results are that it without a doubt works. We might not get what we want today, tomorrow, or even a year from now, but don't stop believing (I know you're singing it now), continue doing the next right thing, put in the work and anything is possible.

If we can learn to practice being positive, we will soon find out that the world has a lot more to offer than we ever knew. Do you think sticking with your selfish glass-half-empty attitude is going to help get you out of your current funk (let's face it, you are reading this book for a reason)? Think again. Negativity breeds negativity. Positivity breeds positivity. It is that simple, I just need you to BELIEVE.

Now, you are probably asking yourself, "Jason, how the hell can I be so positive when X, Y, and Z are occurring in my life?" Look, I get it, I do. Been there, done that. It is not going to be easy so be prepared to fight an uphill battle with obstacles scattered about. The payoff will be worth the battle. You will overcome!

The world ain't all sunshine and rainbows. It's a very mean and nasty place... and I don´t care how tough you are, it will beat you to your knees and keep you there permanently, if you let it. You, me or nobody, is gonna hit as hard as life. But it ain't about how hard you hit... It's about how hard you can get hit, and keep moving forward... how much you can take, and keep moving forward. That´s how winning is done. Now, if you know what your worth, then go out and get what you worth. But you got to be willing to take the hits. And not pointing fingers saying: You ain´t what you wanna be because of him or her or anybody. Cowards do that and that ain´t you! You´re better than that!

- Rocky Balboa -

Do yourself a favor, get on You-tube and type in "Rocky Speech" and enjoy. Do you know the story of Sylvester Stallone? No? Okay, let me brighten your day and feed some hope and inspiration into that mind. Sly, or Rocky, as we all know him by, was just your average Joe, trying to make a career for himself as an actor. His first starring role of his acting career was in soft-core pornography. Yes, you read that right. He had been evicted from his apartment and was potentially facing long-term homelessness, so he did whatever it took to get things moving in the right direction. He certainly could have fell victim to a negative mindset and played the blame game, but Sly chose to do the exact opposite. He received a few minor acting roles throughout the early '70s, and then it happened. After witnessing an Ali fight, he began writing tirelessly on the script that would become *Rocky*. Once finished, he paraded it around

Hollywood looking for someone to take it on, but with a catch: Stallone himself wanted to play the lead role and would not sell his script otherwise. Well, needless to say the rest is history. *Rocky* has gone on to become one of the most decorated movie series of all-time, and for his part, Stallone was inducted into the International Boxing Hall of Fame. The life of Sylvester Stallone is the perfect story of perseverance, determination, believing in yourself, and doing whatever it takes to get what you want, to get what you deserve. Are you up for the challenge?

[2]

Do You Believe in Miracles?

"The future belongs to those who prepare for it today."

- Malcolm X -

If you would like to accomplish something, you must first expect it for yourself. It all starts with a belief. What do you expect for yourself? Do you expect the prosperity in life that you are entitled to *if* you put in the work to earn it? Do you expect to manifest the kind of relationships that you would like? There is nothing as powerful as a changed mind. You must change what's possible for you. There is greatness inside of all of you. Yes, I am talking to YOU! God has given every one of us a gift and it is up to us to decide to share it with the world or not. If you want to succeed you must commit to your gift and embrace it with open arms.

Every day you are going to have people in your life who tell you that you can't and that you are incapable of, from family, to friends, to loved ones. If you are tirelessly working on bettering yourself then you won't even notice the behaviors and opinions of those around you. This is simply called being in "the zone", which any athlete understands as a time where everything slows down for you. If you become so busy in building up your craft you will get lost in those endeavors and that is where we begin to reach our greatest potential. Once you stop and admit to defeat, all those haters will say I told you so. Just keep grindin'. You are the reason you are **not** succeeding, no one else. If you are going to blame him, her, and everyone else for your own mistakes, your downfalls, your struggles, then you better be thanking them for all the good that occurs in your life.

We cannot live with a negative mindset and expect positive results. Most of you are waking up every morning searching for pain, drama, problems, etcetera that are hindering you from becoming successful and happy and you don't even realize it. The majority of unhappy people's first thought of the day is "I didn't get enough sleep" or "I slept like shit!" The negative mindset has begun before they have even got out of bed. Do you really expect your life to be any different and to get any better if you consistently wake up with this mindset? You can change that right now. When you wake up tomorrow morning I want you to find something to be grateful for to set the tone for your day. If you cannot find anything to be grateful for then you clearly are not looking hard enough. *Stop Thinking Like That* ended up in your hands, whether it be the physical copy or on whatever electronic device you have, so right there is something to be grateful for. This book might be the only thing on your list today and that is quite alright. I promise you that your list will grow if you want it to or if you follow through with reading *STLT* until the end.

I personally write my gratitude list each morning upon waking up. This list reminds me of all the precious possessions I already have in life, the blessings that God has given me, and it's also a reminder of what I have lost over time due to my negative belief system. Comedian Steve Harvey feels blessed just for waking up each day. He states he cannot wait to start his morning by spending the first ten minutes of his day lying in bed not addressing any of his life problems, but rather being thankful that he is simply present, and alive. Be thankful, be gracious, and be positive. Change can occur for you today, right now. Steve Angello, of the legendary house music group Swedish House Mafia, opens his song *Rejoice* with "You have to fix the mind before you can bestow the blessings" that are available to you, that you deserve. If you want change then you must change your mindset first. Only you are capable of changing your mind, so the ball is in your court. Are you ready to push forward beyond your limits or have you already thrown in the towel?

"Keep away from those who try to belittle your ambitions."

- Mark Twain -

Your time is limited so please do yourself a favor and do not waste it living anyone else's life. Do not become trapped by dogma and live through others expectations, thoughts, and beliefs. It is a very slippery slope when we put our happiness into others hands. I recently spoke with colleague and author Sarah Ordo about her issue dealing with expectations, in particular during her younger years. Ordo has self-published two fabulous books, *Sober As F*ck* and *Innerbloom*, that speak of recovery and finding your inner happiness. She, like thousands of other teenagers and young adults, relied on outside approval to feel good enough on the inside and for her happiness. She told me that there was pressure from a young age to be perfect and felt pushed to do her best in everything she did, whether it be dance or cheerleading or trying to be the popular 'it' girl. Her confidence relied on the reassurance from others telling her she was going about her life the right way, which, for a teenage girl trying to find her way in the world, is extremely unhealthy.

Living for others is a major reason why depression is increasingly prominent in not only today's youth and teenagers but in adults, as well. *Time* magazine ran a story in August 2017 about depression in America reporting that 13% of citizens in this country were on anti-depressants during a study done from 2011-2014. That figure rose to nearly 65% since the last survey that was reported from 1999-2002. When we don't succeed in life we tend to withdraw from everything and feel less than. No one deserves to feel less than. It is clear why, as we enter the early stages of adulthood, the opinions of others are hard to run from and we safeguard ourselves from failure. Then, when failure inevitably does occur we have no ways to overcome it because of the lack of preparation. That leads us down a scary path, one that I personally have traveled and part of the reason behind writing *Stop Thinking Like That* is to help prevent others from taking that road. We will dive much deeper into failure in the pages ahead, but always remember that NO ONE is excused from experiencing it.

I am telling you do not let the outside noise of others drown out your own inner voice. Your heart and intuition already know what it is you desire to become, so why not follow them? It is a constant struggle we all have worrying about how we are perceived by others, what they may think if we do or don't do this, and what will they think of us if we fail. What if you become someone no one thought you could ever be? What if you shut the mouths of all the haters by backing up your talk by walking the walk? Are you going to let those same people affect what you have accomplished? Affect the happiness YOU have created?

There will *always* be people who do not want to see you succeed. The bigger your dream the bigger the bus needed to carry all of your doubters. The criticism and negative stigmas will only grow with the more action you take. Why? Because by taking this massive action you will begin to experience tremendous success and that will lead to the people below you, the *average*, judging you. This is called envy and you are going to create a lot of it because those stuck in mediocrity cannot stomach witnessing others succeed!

Do not listen to any of the nonsense, just continue to believe in yourself. To live the life that you have always wanted to you must go after your dreams and follow your heart. Do not waste any more time waiting because no one is coming to save your ass and handing you what you want. If you continue to sit back and wait for everything to come to you, then ultimately you will end up living exactly like everyone predicted you would. You will have proved all the doubters and naysayers right. Success and happiness are not going to one day 'poof' and appear like a magic trick. It is up to you to go out and grab it and take what's yours because I know it doesn't feel good when people don't believe in you. It feels even worse when you prove them right. Mark Twain states it best, "The secret of getting ahead is getting started." Pretty simple, right? The only thing holding you back is not getting going which all starts with a simple belief. Conceive it, believe it, and then you WILL achieve it!

[3]

If at First You Don't Succeed

"You miss 100% of the shots you don't take."

- Wayne Gretzky -

I have failed more times in my life than I am proud to admit to. I have failed on the diamond, in the classroom, on the job, in too many relationships to count, as a son, and the list goes on. Failure is and will *always* be an option in everything we do, and our responses to these situations ultimately will determine the affect they have on us. What we need to do is embrace it and immerse ourselves in our failures, so we can learn how to overcome the hurt, pain, and disappointment that comes along with them. When you fail don't worry, instead continue telling yourself "I will not give up! I will keep moving forward!" If you want to change you do not need to accept failure anymore, but only *if* you are willing to change. Change is never easy; as many fear what it may bring, that the grass is *not* greener. But what if you never find out? Not being willing to try is the worst kind of failure there may be. To change, I need you to commit to the process. I need you to commit to everything you do with an obsession, passion, and as the G.O.A.T. Tom Brady would say, with "laser focus".

It is time for you to accept the feeling of being uncomfortable because that is where greatness lies. A good way to become comfortable with being uncomfortable is by practicing it with simple tasks in our daily lives. Don't be scared to go treat yourself to a nice dinner at a restaurant solo. New to working out? Ask the gym you reluctantly joined about working with a personal trainer. Constantly finding yourself gazing out the window daydreaming during every presentation the same monotonous co-worker puts together? Offer to do the presentation the next time. And, please go look into the nearest mirror and say the following out loud; "I love you!" Loving ourselves is an obligatory step to discovering the best version that resides within us all. After you are done pouting and cursing me out for making you feel vehemently uncomfortable, wipe away those pity tears, roll your sleeves up, and let's get to grindin'. As always, you can thank me later.

I know I hated the pain and suffering I felt from all my failures over the years. In order to change my life, I had no choice but to change my thoughts and actions. I decided to do whatever it took in order to never have to experience that unsavory way again. All the pent-up anger inside of me led to a fire burning the inner walls of my belly, begging, pleading, and desiring a change of life. I knew I would have to go to great lengths if I wanted positive change to occur for me. I grew completely tired of being comfortable and content with the depressing life I was living, not caring if this was simply *it* for me. If I were to ever live out the life I had always dreamt of then I had to go back and learn from my past failures, as hard and deflating of the ego it may be, and use those lessons as motivation to succeed moving forward. I knew I had to make a *complete* transformation of myself if I were to ultimately dismiss the stagnant life I was living, which meant changes to my mind, body, and soul. It is your turn to transform yourself and I am going to walk with you every step of the way.

My mind had become accustomed to failure, to defeat, and settled in for the long haul with these delicacies. Action needed to be taken! Thus, I began pushing out all the negative bullshit I had planted in my brain over the years and replaced it with positivity. I knew inside me there was an ambitious, driven, take-no-prisoners individual and that I was not put on this earth to become a self-loathing loser isolating from society by drinking and drugging life's problems away on my couch with all the blinds shut around me. It was time for the light to break through and to fight back. No longer was I going to accept that life. My addictions were not going to win any longer. I got up off my ass and started on the long, but momentous road ahead to recovering the real man I knew that was inside of me just waiting to be unleashed. I am getting goose bumps as I sit here writing this because that was the moment that would forever change my life. That was the moment I took my first step forward.

If you fail while making an attempt at self-betterment that is still progress, no matter the result. Remember, we seek progress in our journey, not perfection. One less attempt is now needed to get to where you want to go, to achieve what you want to achieve. One more failure that you can learn from is now at your disposal, learning what not to do the next time. It is said that after failed attempt 9,999 at refining the light bulb, Edison responded with; "I have not failed. I have just found 9,999 ways that don't work." If you want something then you must be willing to go to any lengths to achieve it. Are you willing to fail 10,000 times to reach your goal? Okay, maybe not 10,000, but I need you to have the whatever-it-takes mentality during this journey. No obstacle is too big, no failure is too deflating, and no outside opinion will alter your plan. You will persevere. You will triumph. You will succeed.

"You can either live your dreams or live your fears."

- Les Brown -

Right now, you have two options; step forward and start your journey or fall back into the safety net of your current mundane existence. The choice is yours. For those of you stepping forward please fasten your safety devices, put your tray tables up, and prepare for takeoff. For the rest of you, your 2nd place trophies should be arriving in the mail soon. I will always be here for you, but until then I am off and running on the winner's bracket side.

Digging yourself out from the bottomless pit that has swallowed you whole is not an easy task. I know how it feels to think that you are doomed forever, and the astronomical effort needed to find the strength and fortitude necessary to start your ascent. I will never forget the demoralization I felt while stuck in the fetal position in the corner of that ghastly pit. The key for me to continuing the difficult push forward and not settling for mediocrity or even worse non-existence was to hold onto the appalling feeling that kidnapped all of my dreams and aspirations, as a reminder. There is no rest once you overcome the adversity that had a firm grasp on your life; we must always press on. Time is limited so we can never stop in our endless pursuit of maximum opportunity and growth, forever furthering ourselves from the adverse situations that *had* full possession of our choices and decisions.

Now that you no longer accept being average, it is time to take action. And massive action at that. A dream is nothing but a dream until we have a plan to accomplish said dream. We need to rewire that brain of yours to rid of all the negative nonsense that has corrupted it for far too long. No longer will you live with that self-defeating attitude thinking you are less than and you can't. You can. You will.

Get off your ass and open those blinds. All it takes is one step forward, right over your previous mere existence because your fresh limitless life starts right NOW. Remember, what the mind can conceive and believe, the mind can achieve. Start to fill your mind with all the things in life you have been missing out on because you were too scared to take that first step. Go after what you always have wanted to achieve. Your dreams are waiting for you now go out and catch them before they are lost forever. Visualize them day and night until you KNOW you will live them out.

What are you scared of? Don't you want to live that life you've always dreamed of? Don't you want to travel to the places you always envisioned visiting? Yes, the bigger our dream and the more success we desire then the more responsibilities that come along with it. You must ask yourself what's more important to you; living out a life to the fullest experiencing as much as you possibly can during the rest of your time on this precious earth or running away and hiding from the extra grit and grind you'll need to put in to take on the new responsibilities? If you choose the latter then I guess you didn't really want that wonderful life for you and your family. I guess you're happy and satisfied living in your little bubble and all those places you envied growing up must not seem so beautiful after all.

Living life in mediocrity might *have been* for you, but you are no longer accepting it as your final destination. This is the only life we get and for me I'm going to experience as much as I possibly can every single day I wake up breathing. No matter the grind, I'm going to bust my ass to make the most of this one opportunity I have on this beautiful planet. I am extremely grateful to have this opportunity, so I have made the decision to waste it no more. It is time to experience life to the fullest as if it is your last damn day on this earth because one day it will be and that day could be today. I want actual proof that all those exotic places I saw in National Geographic's as a kid or seen in movie theaters really do exist, especially the island in *The Beach* that Leo patrols.

For me to visit those places and do exciting things means I must put in some strenuous work and carry the load of those extra responsibilities. Please bring them my way, I am not scared to get my hands dirty! The bigger the dream the harder the task, which to me means I get to see how far I really can take my life. It means I get to push myself to levels I've never been to before. Great! More new experiences of life for me to, well, experience.

Whatever we want we can have, even the foreign lands found in old magazines are available to us. Don't be scared. Pain is temporary, but memories last a lifetime. I hope to see you in Phuket soon!

The Real World

Soon after I graduated college in northern California I moved back to Florida and found myself sitting in a cubicle for a mortgage company. The sub-prime crisis was rearing its ugly head across the country during this time, but there was still a lot of money to be made, especially for a twenty-three-year-old college grad entering his first post-college employment. I truly loved this job from the get go because I was sold on the attitudes of the employees that worked there, particularly the managements. The owner of the company, which had branches across the state of Florida, had the absolute most positive outlook on life of anyone I had ever met and I knew I wanted that.

This job taught me a lot of valuable lessons during my two years working there, for better and worse. One lesson I learned from jump street was that I had the opportunity to make a lot of money, more money than a kid who six months prior was sitting in an 8am Biomedical Ethics lecture knows what to do with. I got into the business as the sub-prime crisis was starting to rip overzealous Americans lives completely apart. All this meant was I would be working with more qualified applicants making the four to six-week process smooth as Skippy. As quick and near-harmless as a refinance or purchase could go I would still need to put in the time and effort to achieve what I had set out to.

This is where I learned the concept of the cream rising to the top. There always seemed to be three or four brokers from our Orlando and West Palm Beach branches that were consistently standing atop the podium like they were healthy wealthy Adonis'. Always dressed to impress, they clearly had put a lot of hard work into chiseling their physiques and could talk an Eskimo into buying ice for his igloo. I wanted what they had and I knew I'd have to take massive action to do so.

The positive attitudes and confident gaits started at the top with our company president and founder. A bowling ball figure who contested in Mr. Florida competitions, with a hint of Asia-Pacific skin topped with a smile that could light up a funeral parlor. It was very clear that this man had the "it" factor. I may have wanted the status that the slick brokers conveyed, but I desired to have the life that our owner lived. My immediate goal was to become one of the top brokers in the company. My long-term goal was much grander; to be the assiduous go-getter with the beautiful family, large home, running multiple highly successful companies. To achieve this, I had to raise my work ethic to levels above and beyond what anyone else was representing, including the owner.

The drive to be the best mortgage broker I could possibly be was on as I began watching intently, extremely listening (listening deeply to strengthen and expand our emotional intelligence helping form better relationships) and emulating the daily grind of those I was striving to be. My branch's general manager saw the fire in my eyes and that I possessed that "it" factor, but I would need guidance to help lead me to those grander pastures. She began the process of teaching me about one of the main concepts of this book; a positive mindset. Out came the literature that would begin the transformation of my mind, my attitude, and my perspective on life as a whole. For Christmas during my first year with the company she bought me a book called *Success Through a Positive Mental Attitude* by W. Clement Stone & Napoleon Hill. Soon after, I bought Hill's *Think & Grow Rich* as well as a Tony Robbins book that one of the other branches managers recommended. Before I knew it, I had completely bought into the philosophies these books unearthed and I became a glutton for this newfound mindset, feeding my brain positivity for breakfast, lunch, and dinner.

By May of that following year I had risen to the top...of my branch in Tampa. On my birthday at the end of that month I found myself driving my dream car (story to come), but the icing on the cake came at the company's annual summer outing at a water park in Orlando. At this event, the Gatsbian owner had a presentation for his top sales producers by amount of revenue they brought in for the first two quarters of the year. I ended up finishing as one of the top five employees companywide and I was there to stay. I was no longer some jayvee call-up, I was now on the starting squad alongside the elite. With the recognition on stage also came an all-inclusive trip to Jamaica with all the top brass from each branch. Hard work pays off, just keep grindin'.

The qualities to become a successful individual out in the real world were now embedded into my cranium. To make their stay permanent I can never rest on my laurels and must continue surrounding myself with winners! I am extremely grateful for my manager willingly taking me under her wing to show me what it took to be the best. The characteristics I learned throughout those two years working under her fortunately for me did not crawl away and disappear during my decade long drive on the highway to hell. I would uncover them once again in the years to come. Be on the lookout.

Mother of Pearl

One of the books I read during my mind's transformation stage suggested an unusual exercise about how to get the things we wish to have. It starts by visualizing what you aspired to possess, what you wished to obtain in life, by surrounding yourself with images of these things, whether it be taping them to your bathroom mirror, pinning them to your desk at work, or next to your key rack so it is the last thing your brain views as you head out the door. I knew the aspect of visualization had clearly worked for many before me and figured what is the worst that could happen? I took the silly suggestion and printed up a few photos of the car I beautified over at the time, but was a pipe dream that I could one day call my own;

an Infiniti G35 coupe. My mind could not escape the pictures of this beauty, constantly being reminded what I intensely desired and it soon became imperative that I purchase one. As soon as I turned my computer on at the office there it was in the background; a majestic pearl white G35.

The visualizing of the car subconsciously pushed me to grind harder than I ever had, motivating me to make those extra calls, work late hours, and go into an empty office on Saturdays. A few months down the road on my 25th birthday I bought myself a shiny pearl white Infiniti G35 coupe driving her right off the dealership floor. Once the grin on my face wore off, the real message came to light. Anything is achievable if we truly put our minds to it and follow through with the necessary work. Whatever it takes. The value of the hard work was sealed after I saw the look on my parents faces the first time they saw my new purchase. It was a proud moment that left me with a feeling I knew I could not live without and it all started with a visualization. That is the power of a positive mind. And I became addicted to it. What is it in life that you cannot live without, but do not yet possess? What have you always dreamed of having?

The love I had for that vehicle and the work I put into keeping her looking pristine was like a mama tiger constantly lathering up her cubs. I was extremely proud to be driving her around (yes, my cars are all women) for it showed the unstoppable work ethic I possessed as well as being undeterred by other's opinions. Many of my co-workers were in disbelief that first day I pulled into our office's parking garage in my silk beauty. In the couple months prior their eyes would roll as they walked by my cubicle with a snicker when they saw the pictures I had plastered all over my desk area, from the screen saver to my cork board. I knew I was destined to earn the right to purchase her as did my boss.

Her continuous words of encouragement inspired and motivated me to persist steadfastly in my pursuit of this goal of attaining my first new vehicle that I could call my own. My focus was solely on the task at hand, not on the weak-minded co-workers and their discouraging words nor the amount of action that would need to be taken to acquire the car and leave my fellow employees mouths gaping wide. I was on a mission that became more than buying a fancy new car, but about proving to myself what was possible if I were to fully commit to my word. The lesson taught from this experience was more than just pure vindication. I now had personal proof that I can do whatever I put my mind to as long as I am willing to put in the time and effort. My mom's words never rang so true than at that moment.

What Goes Up

The learning process did not come to a halt after I drove my new car off the dealership lot. The joy of success soon led to the humiliation that can accompany failure. A couple of years after my purchase I was abruptly awoken in the middle of the night by the sound of an angry car alarm. Upon sprinting out the door into the humid Florida evening, I saw my favorite girl being held in the clutches of a tow truck and she soon became a distant sight. The lesson learned here was how quickly the things we work so hard for can be taken away from us if we become complacent and lose perception of how we have got to where we are. This unfortunate incident was all due to my own doing. Instead of partaking in the proper adult etiquette of bill-paying, I chose to chase the euphoric high that pain killers had brought to my life. Talk about having my priorities straight, huh? Like I said from the onset, I managed to lose everything during my destructive journey in addiction. No matter how much we think we like/love/adore someone or something, nothing seems to be able to stand up to the made-up mind of an addict. It takes tremendous courage to ask for help, but when you do I promise things will get better. You are not alone. Ever.

To the contrary, when your mind has made up that you no longer will accept your current way of living, whether it be in addiction, laziness and procrastination, or lack of progression, then change must take place. If we truly want this change to occur in our lives, we need to be agreeable to change ourselves and that starts with being open and willing. Look to new ideas that have seamlessly worked for many of the greats before you and around you today. If putting a picture of the John Deere tractor you have always gawked at, but felt you could never obtain will help you finally get the chance to buy one then damn it go find all the pictures of that green machine you can and post them everywhere! Feed your mind that which you desire.

It is time to pour yourself into your endeavors and pursue them with the absolute best you can muster up. There are no shortcuts to get to the summit; you will have to trudge through the muck to arrive at your destiny. But let me tell you this; the juice is absolutely worth the squeeze. Sacrificing happy hour with the girls for a barre class will benefit you much more than the three glasses of vino you will be consuming. Sleeping through your mornings on the weekend only gives your competition that much more time to go after what you say you want, but you don't back up your talk with the walk. Only you know how much time you are wasting by laying around in bed all day; wasting away the opportunity to get better and grow. There isn't much productivity occurring as you are swiping right on Tinder or liking every kitty post on Facebook. When you wake up with a purpose you can then decide what it is you can do today that will help you inch that much closer to where you want to go tomorrow. Every day you have the opportunity to get closer to your ultimate destination, don't waste them.

If you want change then you must be willing to make some sacrifices, big and small. The changes that you must make to manifest the life you are entitled to might be straining and strenuous and take time to notice. Just keep grindin'. One healthy habit after another will soon lead to your life changing without you even being aware. That is the beauty of it. You are in control of everything you do. As long as you keep doing the work, no matter the difficulty it brings, good positive things will happen to you and your life. There are no ceilings or limitations to what we are capable of when we are resilient in our actions to overcoming whatever adversity we are facing. If we truly want something there are no limits so please do not sell yourself short. It is time for you to see what the unconditional best version of you is capable of. Only you know when you lay your head down at night that you have given your best. Anything less and you're just cheating yourself. The grind never stops!

Always do your best, never stop moving ahead and you will no longer be restricted by the perceived barriers you think are holding you back. You will not be stopped! If your heart desires it and your mind knows it then all you must do is take that first step, and continue grinding forward, one foot in front of the other. Have you noticed a common theme here, yet? All it takes to begin on your path to achieving the ultimate success that you desire is putting one foot forward. The first step to going somewhere is deciding to not stay where you are. If you believe you can, you will. If I did it then so can YOU and I know you are ready so let's take that first step together!

The last weekend of 2017 is upon us and I'm sure everyone is scattering around trying to think of a New Year's resolution to make for 2018. Well, I am here to tell you to stop the scattering. Why must you wait for when the calendar turns over to go after the things that you want today? That you want right now? Do you not want to make the most of the last days of each year and have momentum going into the new one? If you want to start getting better then you need to stop waiting around for a silly ball to drop and get your dang self-going. Before you know it, it's going to be mid-February and you're going to be kissing those resolutions goodbye, if you even remember what they were in the first place. Opportunities will continue to pass you by as you're sitting around waiting for some type of miracle to happen. That miracle is you getting off your couch and putting your ass into high gear to work to get better in whatever endeavor you're after or whatever goal you wish to obtain. If you continue to do what you've always done then you'll continue to get the results you've always gotten. So, let's go and start that resolution right now and we'll all be entering 2018 like a locomotive full steam ahead. It all starts right now.

[4]

Full Speed Ahead

"If you fail to plan, you're planning to fail."

- Benjamin Franklin -

As we previously stated, a dream is nothing but a dream until you have a plan to accomplish it. Once you have a plan then you are ready to get to work. You are no longer a spectator in your own life; you have entered the field of battle. You believe you can and you will. It is time for you to commit to your vision with passion and determination. Obstacles will undoubtedly come up along the way and we will learn how to combat them together. Failure is inevitable, but in order to achieve the greatest level of success in your life you must first go through failure. Just keep grindin'.

If you are continuously taking the necessary action to turn that frown upside down and have buried that negative self-defeating attitude, then you are already working the process. If you want something bad enough you are required to be relentless. Unplanned variables are going to spontaneously show up time and again, but they are what help us build perseverance to keep pushing forward. As I always like to say, "Life happens!"

I recently read a very intriguing article in *Inc.* magazine titled "Decoding the DNA of the Entrepreneur" discussing entrepreneurship. The article speaks about what drives, motivates, and characterizes entrepreneurs, all of which we will dive deeper into down the line in the chapter on winners. *Inc.* surveyed 211 business owners across an array of industries. Not surprisingly four of the top five characteristics of the men and women surveyed were hard-working, competitive, confident and determined. Number four was being a problem-solver, a topic we will touch on soon.

Two of the survey questions went hand-in-hand, discussing one of the major differences between go-getters like you and me (entrepreneurs and winners) and settlers (those content living an average life). The biggest difference: risk. As we will get into later, those looking to chase after their dreams and aspirations do not fear putting all their chips into the middle. The opportunity for greatness is of far more worth to them than the pain of short-term failure.

Of the participating business owners, 61% sight the "willingness to take risks" as the number one reason for their success followed closely by 51% agreeing that "the ability to persevere when times get tough" as the driving force behind their success. Winners are not scared when the going gets tough, instead they buckle up their chinstraps a little tighter and fight on. And if they fail? They step back to assess the situation to see what went wrong using their failure as a learning experience. Do you have what it takes to be a winner? Are you willing to go all-in for the opportunity to live the life you've always envisioned you would?

Mike Beatrice is one of those individuals willing to take the risks necessary to reap the ultimate rewards. Mike and I grew up together, running amuck as teammates on the baseball diamond, football field, and basketball court. He and his family left Massachusetts in sixth grade for a business move out to northern California. We reconnected once Zuck got Facebook up and running, which happened to occur as I was finishing my collegiate days up in northern California.

Always the grinder who'd stick his nose into any endeavor, Mike got the entrepreneurial bug passed down to him from his father. In 2014 Mike put the finishing touches on his beautiful gym in Oakland, California called *The Oakland Fitness Company*. Within a short amount of time, what he coined as "The Movement" became the *It* spot to train in the Bay area for anyone looking to improve their overall health by focusing on fitness, nutrition, and one's lifestyle. His new-age dynamic fitness center was only the beginning of "The Movement", as Mike went on to establish two highly successful businesses within the food industry, of which his father earned much of his success in. *Home Grown Oakland* coincides with his focus on the nutritional side of health, by providing healthy comfort food to help fuel your mind and body. His latest venture, *Side-Show Kitchen*, gives the customer a laid-back neighborhood feel and localized grown food and brew options. Following in the footsteps of *The Oakland Fitness Co.*, both are big hits within the Oakland community.

With three successful business ventures under his belt at just 34 years old, one might think Mike would settle down to reap the benefits of his hard work. But entrepreneurs and winners do not have time to settle down, they continuously grind to become even more successful. Yes, of course he has enjoyed the benefits of being an efficacious entrepreneur, allowing him many joyful times with his family and friends, but the work to be great never stops.

When I asked Mike what drives him to continue pressing on amidst his current run of triumphs and the inevitability of adversity, he delivered the following powerful message; "To excel in any field we must push ourselves to be great. We cannot shy away from our competition or our fears. What we do in the face of the storm is what separates those who are successful versus those who are not. I will say that it is true not everyone has gone through the same struggle to become successful. It is just very likely that at some point there must have been something that challenged a successful person to quit or to consider accepting failure." This is coming from the mouth of a winner with that *just keep grindin'* attitude who didn't crumble in the face of adversity.

In chapter three I told you that you have two choices; "step forward and start your journey or fall back into the safety net of your current mundane life." Mike knew that he wasn't here to be living in mediocrity and settle into an average life at best, so he stepped forward. He recognized he could summon up more potential if only he were willing to put in the effort necessary and that those capabilities could lead him to achieving greatness. Mike wanted to create a better life not only for himself, but for his family. And he knew in order to do so he needed to attack life and do absolutely whatever it takes.

We further went on to exchange our views on what I like to call the *outside noise.* His opinion was spot on with mine; "Do not let any one person or their negative opinion detour you from chasing your dreams. Don't allow anyone to talk you out of something you believe in or have passion and fire for. Those who have not taken the jump and risked it all may find it hard to relate. This is fear; I fear failure much more than I fear risk."

Remember, the bigger our dream, the riskier we are, the more the people around us are going to think we are delusional. That is fine, they cannot see themselves beyond being average, but you and I most certainly can. These people are the ones who accept living in mediocrity and are the hardest ones to change, requiring the most help. They need to be waiting at the door for the mailman to arrive with this book and once they open it up they will soon hear directly from the source that anything is possible with the right mind set and work ethic. As the success you have created begins to build as will the number of haters coming out of the woodwork. Great! That is additional fuel for the fire. Press on, continue to climb, and you will make yourself proud, I promise.

Don't forget, as you begin to make that march on to your new life full of happiness and success be prepared for an army of people attempting to hold you back and disrupt your vision. Anyone who is taking you further away from your goals and dreams must go, no matter who it is. They are stuck with the undesirable trait of possibility blindness and cannot see beyond what they already have, which is nothing but a mediocre existence. That is their choice, not yours. You my friend are striving for greatness!

Your success is like a spotlight shining down on all of your haters' missed opportunities. Let them all sulk in their own misery while you build your empire of happiness. Soon they will be coming to you asking how, envious of your newfound success and joy. Give them your copy of this book. Better yet, tell them to go out and purchase their own so all parties benefit. Hey, I still have loads of debt to pay off from all those years I spent living in inferiority. Now, I am envisioning an abundance of copies selling all across the globe due to your successes.

If I listened to all my doubters I would have never met you. But I believed. Then I took the first step and have tirelessly worked my ass off since, never looking back. One naysayer after the next got crossed off and soon I was only surrounded by winners. Winners know what it takes to be great and have the positive mentality you need to succeed. True winners seek greatness and that is what awaits you if you believe in yourself which I need you to do starting right now. Not tomorrow, not next week, but right now!

[5]

The Past

"Don't judge yourself by your past, you're not living there anymore."

-Anonymous-

I have endlessly pursued greatness and the winning mentality by researching hours on end, reading and studying books written by the people whom I want to emulate, and watching countless motivational You-Tube videos every day. I was and am not going to be denied! Through this research, from those I have interviewed, and from my own personal experiences it was very clear of one thing that can cause us to never get our feet off the ground and will leave us in a stifling pejorative state: the past. We all have them, good, bad, or indifferent, and far too many people allow theirs to completely take a stranglehold of their present.

Living in the past will suck the energy and will out of you quicker than you can brush your teeth, which to you I say you are welcome. You can thank me later for those fresh clean teeth. When we get stuck in our past we immobilize our future. There is nothing wrong with taking a glance into our past, but we cannot get caught staring. When we stare is when trouble starts brewing because we begin to create a negative mindset. One simply cannot live in their past while attempting to progress forward toward their goals. It is humanly impossible to be in two places at one time. You can, however, be occupying four states at once; just ask Google.

Living in our past works hand in hand with our fear of failure. You think "I failed once why should I expect a different outcome this time around"? Joe Manganiello, star of True Bloods and both box office hits, Magic Mike & Magic Mike XXL, wrote about how he overcame his failures to become the uber-talented actor he now is in his book *Evolution*, stating "I was brought down by previous failures and preconceived notions about what I could become. I unknowingly set myself up to fail time after time." He further goes on to explain how he "had to learn how to overcome some massive difficulties along the way" showing us that no one is exempt from the challenges of life. No matter if you are a multimillion-dollar actor, a professional athlete, a school teacher, or unemployed, failure is part of the process to bettering your life. It is up to us how we choose to fight back to overcome these hardships. The unsuccessful people in this world are spending the majority of their time and energy dwelling on their past while fantasizing about their future as the winners are taking immediate action and continuing to succeed by seeing their past mistakes and failures as opportunities for growth.

To reiterate the failure factor: it is absolutely necessary to experience failure before you can succeed. Just imagine if Edison quit trying in his bid for electricity you would be reading this book with a lantern by your side. How about if his airness Michael Jordan abandoned his dream of playing in the NBA because he was cut his sophomore year of high school? What if your parents gave up trying to get a pair of chromosomes to come together? Sorry for the visual now stuck in that cranium of yours. The point is that everyone fails and those who succeed do not give up once the failure blood is drawn. They bandage that shit up, sharpen their swords, and are back trudging through the muck, this time with a bigger arsenal of tools in their *Just Keep Grindin'* toolbox.

Not only does living in the past restrain us from progressing forward, it also embeds all the negative thoughts and feelings from our past deeper into our mind. We will expand much more on negative versus positive mind sets as we dig deeper into the power behind positivity. These two negatives certainly are not turning anything positive anytime soon.

Your past has already happened; you cannot take it back nor can you change a thing about it. What you can do is change your attitude and your thoughts to help better prepare yourself for similar situations that arise moving forward. By making these changes you can find out what needs to be done differently to assure you'll never be where you were again. Personally, I knew with certitude that I could **never** go back to that dreadful, lonely, depressing life I had previously inhabited, and the only thing to guarantee that was by changing ME. No person, place, or thing was going to make that happen, only I was.

Tell yourself you will not be denied. You will work harder than the person next to you. You will seek out and find what you are truly capable of. You will say yes to the late nights. You will say yes to the early mornings. You will do whatever it takes. This is where the opportunities to a better life ascend and you begin to learn as much as possible about yourself. You learn that you are no longer a backward-looking person anymore so please let go. Your future is far too important to be held back by fear. How bad do you want it?

Glory Days

The idea of living in the past is not only unique to the suffering, hurting, depressed, hopeless and all of the negative Nancys out there. Living in your glory days is just as poisonous. I am talking to you Johnny High School. Congratulations on all those accolades accumulated while you were applying Oxy Creme to your face every night. How is that working out for you as you are taking your talents into adulting? I can tell you first hand it is irrelevant that you were the captain of your high school football team or the class president.

I was inducted into one of Massachusetts' most elite high school athletic Hall of Fames in 2016. I entered adulthood thinking I was invincible and that everything was going to come easy to me just like I was accustomed to back in my hay day. Thankfully, I did go to that prominent high school that prepares you for the transition into the next realm of life, but that didn't stop me from eventually losing everything I had ever worked for. I put in the bare minimum of effort in most of my endeavors, becoming complacent by thinking my talent alone would take me to the top and ultimately my ego got the best of me. We need to always remind ourselves that who we were is NOT who we are moving forward, no matter how good or how bad we may have been. There will *always* be room for improvement in all facets of life.

Our egos can be as dangerous for our growth as a negative mindset can, if not worse. We cannot rest on our laurels and expect life to always translate the way we want it to. Life is changing all around us each day and those who continue to find joy and success are the ones changing along with it. They know the competition is not sitting around playing video games twenty-four seven, unless of course they are a gamer by trade. Everyone is always gunning for you, so if you are content and settled with who you *have been* then you will undoubtedly leave yourself vulnerable to have everything you have ever worked for pulled right out from underneath you. Do not accept that you have reached your capacity for success and happiness. Do not ever settle and stop striving for greatness because if you want to be a champion in life you must continuously be determined and motivated to achieve more. We must always fight the fight.

Our past is not only full of suffering and tragedy. The positive events and achievements we have accomplished can help in our future growth by learning from those successes exactly like we must do with our failures. Our successes teach us what we are capable of doing and build up our confidence. What you have achieved in your life thus far is nothing to slouch over. There is nothing wrong with being proud of all your victories up to this point in the game, you just cannot be satisfied. It is important to give yourself recognition when it is earned. However, we cannot get caught up on the success we have had in our past and assume positive events will continue for us. Do not think that because you have garnered a few accolades that success will automatically occur again. Remember, the push toward greatness is a life-time commitment. Are you going to commit yourself to the forever process of growing toward limitless prosperity or are you going to live in mediocrity, full of excuses as to why you are where you are? The choice is yours.

Waiting is not an option if we want to be great, to be successful, and to find joy in everyday living. Although I am Irish, I know luck has nothing to do with any of the success I have in my life. Everything we receive in life is earned through hard work, determination, and disciplining ourselves to be consistent. Luck is the byproduct of putting these characteristics into use on a daily basis. Things tend to fall the right way for the men and women who are tireless in their pursuit to better themselves, not for the clock-watcher, the piker, or the lazy sloth. It is often the "unlucky" ones who we see constantly complaining about their bosses, landlords, exes, and making up excuses for their circumstances, that whine about the success seemingly occurring to everyone around them. Luck is not going to find its way onto the couch that's more like a Tempurpedic with your assprint engraved in it. Get up and start to make your own luck by taking action.

Leggo My Ego

Our egos all too often are in the way of our progression toward where we want to go or what we want to get out from underneath of. Speaking as an alcoholic, the ego is one of the main reasons why we do not seek the help we desperately need. And that goes for all human beings, not just those with addiction problems. It is the kryptonite for change. We believe we are too good to listen to others and are perpetually doing what we have always done then we wonder why we never get to where we want to go. We cannot let anyone know that we need help and fear we'll be seen as weak if we ask for it, so we bottle all these feelings up inside. The reason we hide our problems traces back to the main ingredient that is holding us back in every area of life: *fear.* Fear is everywhere and in everyone and deserves its own chapter, so be prepared to face it sooner than later.

As a twenty something year old, I thought I knew it all, from how to run a relationship to how to manage someone else's company to the next question on Jeopardy. What I really knew was how to ruin relationships, how to disappoint a lot of bosses, and that being in the National Honor Society in high school does not qualify me to be a contestant on this country's greatest game show. Basically, I became an expert at being in the dog house.

No one likes a know-it-all, yet it seems we all are one at some point in our lives. Or maybe that was just me, I don't know? Either way, when we act as if we know everything what we are really doing is putting a pair of tunnel vision goggles on, completely disregarding and ignoring that which is in our peripherals. The information that is available to us in our peripherals is part of the process to arriving at the vision at the end of the tunnel. You cannot drive up to Maine in the fall without witnessing all the foliage in New Hampshire. What that means is that the things around us are all part of our journey to the ultimate destination. Just imagine driving without your side view mirrors. Objects will not be closer than they appear, they will not appear at all and the next thing you know you are sideswiping a group of Hells Angels in the lane over. And you do not want to be the guy knocking down Hells Angels in route to Sturgis. Or anywhere for that matter.

[6]

It's Good to Be Great

"What happens in life echoes in eternity."

- Gladiator -

How do you envision your life five years from now? Where do you see yourself in ten years? How do you want to be remembered when all is said and done? These were the questions my step-father asked me upon finishing my last days of college out in northern California. Five years from now? I could not tell you what I would be doing in five minutes, how could I possible think five years ahead? If only I heeded his advice, then who knows where my life would have led me? I certainly would not have the pleasure of talking to you and for that I am grateful for the ignorance of that twenty-three-year-old.

But the reality is the majority of successful people we come across share the same common traits and answering these questions are an integral part to achieving their goals and sustaining greatness.

My step-father did not build a successful international business from the ground up by just winging it. He put his goals on paper, made both a short and long-term game plan, and followed through with whatever was necessary to make those goals come to fruition. He didn't just put maximum effort into his work when he was feeling at the top of his game. It is the times where we feel like lying in bed all day, the times we are not feeling 100%, the days we cannot find the motivation, that make the difference between being average and having greatness within our grasps. If you want to reach that next level then you need to have an all-or-nothing attitude at all times NO MATTER WHAT! This was a pretty simple concept for me because I already knew I had what it takes to produce maximum effort. I had been going all-in in my efforts to finding the high I required every day from alcohol and drugs for years. There is zero giving up in the search for a high the minute the mind decides it desires drugs. The infatuation causes maximum effort, no matter what.

What is greatness and how do we get there? We cannot strive for something if we are not clear on what it means to us. Everyone will have a different answer to defining greatness, but we are going to go with a collaboration of things that I believe best exemplify how we can arrive at this sought-after attribute.

To achieve greatness, you must go above and beyond what it takes to be at a standstill on common ground with everyone else. You need to elevate yourself above the rest of the pack. There must be a relentless pursuit to honing your craft to the point that only YOU can claim it, no one else. You will need to continuously push forward to get better every day. You must be willing to trudge through the worst terrains, climb the rockiest mountains, crawl, kick, bleed, and cry until you have reached the point where you can proudly stand up and scream, "I did it!" When you have earned the respect not of others, but of yourself, then you my friend have achieved *greatness.*

We all have dreams and I am not talking about the ones that occur in our sleep. As kids we were always told to *dream big* and that we can be anything we want to be. But why does it seem that as we get older and enter the adult world those dreams and aspirations are drastically diminished to simply just getting by? I understand that life happens, and certain events will affect the direction we ultimately go, but that does not mean we suddenly give up on our dreams and settle.

I Want You!

What is it that you want in life? What made you walk into the self-help or recovery section of the bookstore, grab a copy of *Stop*

Thinking Like That, and bring it up to the register at the bookstore or made you click the Buy Now button on Amazon? What is it that is missing from your life? What are you searching for? When you can answer these questions honestly then you will be able to take the next step and set-up a plan, beginning with writing everything down.

I don't expect everyone to be like myself and dare I say all the successful person contained in these pages by having a pen and notebook handy at all times, but I suggest you do. Thousands of thoughts and ideas pop into our minds throughout the day, freely coming and going. By carrying around a pen and paper you can write down the important thoughts that come about at any time. I can say I am guilty of not always adhering to this concept. When I am walking to and from the library to write this book, listening to motivational videos, my mind fills with a myriad of amazing ideas and words structured into blissful paragraphs of which I wish I could tell you, but I continue walking. I know that whatever I remember is what was meant to be put down on paper. The chosen words that make up these pages are exactly what is meant for you to read.

The next page is for you to take advantage of by writing out the first thoughts that come to mind when you ponder the above questions. Make a bulletin or write them out in paragraph form. Either way put your answers and thoughts on paper so you can see for yourself what you desire and feel. See for yourself what it is you desire.

____

____

____

____

____

____

____

____

S.M.A.R.T.

There is a very well-known method of goal setting called S.M.A.R.T. which stands for specific, measurable, attainable, relevant, and time-sensitive. Once you have your specific goals, grab a pen and paper and write them down, big and bold. Go ahead, I will wait. There is tremendous power behind writing down our goals and seeing them on paper. Putting pen to paper is an intimate experience and the things you write down become a part of you from here on out. A bond is forming and we do not even know it. This is the beginning of achieving the success you have always envisioned obtaining. From your own place to call home, a cruise around the Mediterranean, or getting promoted at your job, all of these start with a simple vision and proceeding to step forward.

> **Writer's Note**: I am not completely sold on the **A** in the acronym, as you will notice throughout the book. However, I will acknowledge that the small attainable goals are necessary to successfully navigate through to achieve the bigger goals that turn others' heads. Those are the goals that lead us to greatness, the ones that I am eluding to when I speak passionately about the goals we set. I expect the smaller reasonable ones to be crushed along your drive to the top. Check that, I already know you will crush them!

Remember the more we visualize that which we desire the more our mind is working behind the scenes to achieve it. Of course, simply writing down our goals and visualizing them does not equate to a sudden solution. There is a lot of work to be put in, but you are now positively changing your mindset which is the starting point for self-improvement. This is you taking that first step! When setting your goals, you should feel the excitement rush through your bones and the anxiety trying to burst out of your body, all amped up to get moving. Go ahead and close your eyes and imagine driving that dream car, laying on a beach in Ibiza, getting the keys to your family's new home, or better yet I want you to envision waking up next to the love of your life with a smile.

Your dreams are your dreams so please do not hold back and dream big like you are seven years old again. And I am not talking about the big wheels you always wanted, but hey, you do you. There are no limits to what you can attain; anything you want is yours for the taking. But if we set minimal goals that don't excite us, then we will act as if they were insignificant in the first place when any sign of adversity that comes along. Lack of passion will make it that much easier to give up once we run into a roadblock. If you are not eager to chase after your goals then there will be lack of motivation which is why it's necessary to set higher goals, not easily achievable ones. Give your mind a reason to want to go on the attack with enthusiasm and fire. Otherwise this will ultimately lead to you becoming accustomed with failure and not taking responsibility for not succeeding. You will find yourself saying about your goal, "It wasn't really important anyways." That attitude is not allowed by any of my readers, no questions asked. We are all doers!

When setting your goal(s) be sure to up your game and do not ever short-change yourself. One of my original goals during my adult years has always been to write a book. Pretty standard and realistic as basically this only requires me to become disciplined enough to sit down and put words on paper. Certainly not an easy task, but one that is very reasonable. However, I know I am capable of much more than just writing a book, something anyone can do if they just sit down and write. I raised my standards and now strive to not only write a book, but to write a New York Times bestselling book. Therefore, I knew I must increase my production and take massive action if I wanted to soon be identified as a bestselling author.

Worst case scenario is I achieved my original goal of writing a book. See how that works? Think of it this way; would you rather have a $100,000 or $1,000? Easy answer, so why not strive to achieve the greater amount? This way if you come up short, you are still going to have a thousand more reasons to smile.

If you see someone living the life that you are longing for you now have proof that it is *possible* that you too can live that life. Or why not better? Anything someone else has already accomplished can be achieved once again when the necessary work is put in. Others' achievements only confirm what I already have a strong conviction for and that is that nothing is impossible. Nearly every great idea has been born from an outlandish thought against the norm. Today we are using iPhone X's to basically run our daily activities thanks to the innovative ideas of Steve Jobs. You can go shopping for that retro-leather jacket you always wanted on Facebook, a site originally created to link college students on select campuses across the US.

People I have met in the past few months have called me crazy, delusional and who know what else behind my back, as I continue to pedal my ass down to the library multiple times a day to passionately add thousands of words in my quest to fulfilling my goal of becoming a bestselling author. I love and embrace the disparagement because every day I know I am getting that much closer to my goal, further fueling my drive. With each passing moment I know I am reassuring myself of my commitment to my purpose in life and for the passion that compels me to inspire. I just keep grindin'.

Visualization is a key component for anyone attempting to be successful in their endeavors, particularly with athletes. I practiced the art of visualization before every single at-bat I took from my college days in Florida and California into my professional career. I would stand in the on-deck circle with laser focus on the pitcher, from his mechanics, his mannerisms, his tells, to his delivery. I would then take practice swings in unison with the delivery as if I were the batter up at the plate, helping perfect my timing. Finally, I would close my eyes and envision the end result of my at-bat, which undoubtedly would be me lining a laser beam up the middle knocking the pitcher down to the dirt. I knew if I could have that laser focus then the rest is like riding a bicycle; I would lead, and the muscles would naturally follow.

Did I envision knocking a ball over the light post in right center instead of a line drive up the middle from time to time? Absolutely! I was a middle of the order power bat, so that was a huge part of my success as a baseball player. However, by focusing on lacing a single up the middle I could make the necessary adjustment to any pitch coming my way without thinking about it.

If you are thinking while you are at the plate, the pitcher has already defeated you. Hitters need to get to the point where they react instead of thinking. I would always say to my players on the teams I coached to "Don't think, just do", a spinoff of what one of my high school coaches repetitively said to us, "Relax, good hitter." Your natural instincts take over and if you have done the proper visualizing while waiting on the on-deck circle then you are in good position to win the one on one battle against the man opposing you on the rubber.

For me, that would mean everything was working as one from my hands to my hips to my eyes. I was like a well-oiled machine on these occurrences and more often than not that ball ended up on the other side of the outfield fence. Visualization is a necessary part of the process, whether it be for athletes, for reaching your weekly quota, for hitting new personal bests at the gym, to walking into a showroom to buy that beautiful care you've always dreamed of driving.

Be very precise and direct with your goals. If we are too vague with what we want then we don't give our mind the chance to focus on the specifics which ultimately leads to vague results. We want our mind to know exactly what it is that we desire. I was very specific when my goal at twenty-four years old was to buy myself that pearl white Infiniti G35 coupe. This allowed my subconscious to begin to hyper-focus on the idea of me driving that specific car. It was then up to me to do my part by putting in the time and effort to acquire it. It is all warm and fuzzy obsessing over this amazing life we wish to live, but if you want to make this obsession a reality you must take massive action.

When your goal is specific, measurable, realistic, and attainable then it is time to set up the date for when you want to have it accomplished by. Myself, I have my goals written down in accords to months, starting with the immediate future. What can you do today to help get you that much closer to achieving your ultimate goal? You can start working toward the goals you have written down at this very moment. Well, after you finish this chapter as I don't want to swindle you of all the necessary ammunition to succeed. Once you have fully committed to achieving your goals then from there on out it becomes natural to take the necessary actions without thinking. Your habit is formed, and you will now be machine-like in your efforts.

Our goal is realistic and true, so now it's time to begin the process. Let's say we have a goal to become debt free within the next year. We know we cannot pay it all off at once or we wouldn't have it in the first place, so we need to game plan on how to begin to cut away at the debt. The first step to taking action is to break our goals down into small manageable chunks with a completion date. For this example, we will have $12k worth of debt that we would like to have paid off within a year. That $12k can be broken into saving a $1,000 a month. The thought of trying to find an extra grand lying around each month is still an intimidating figure so let's go even further and see what we need to sock away per week. This allows our mind to have a more direct vision and it can begin to hyper-focus on the task at hand. Breaking a day or week down is much more manageable and far less overwhelming than focusing on the overall objective amount. Trying to come up with roughly $33 a day keeps our stress levels down which means less chance of adding another prescription bottle to our already stocked medicine cabinet. Start breaking down what you want to achieve into small manageable chunks and you are on your way to fulfilling that goal.

[7]

No Matter What

"Be so good they can't ignore you."

- Steve Martin -

No matter who you are or what you are doing, there will be toxic people discouraging you from achieving your dreams. The critics are and will always be present. I welcome all the doubters that need to be taking notes rather than giving glares, because I will not stop anytime soon forever leaving vacancy on that Greyhound for them. Keep in mind as your doubters increase your success is increasing as well. The more criticism you receive the more powerful and successful you are becoming. Envy is now cementing its place into all of those who have doubted, picked on, and called you out. The accomplishments that happen in your life from grindin' day in and day out will be more rewarding with every single mouth you shut. Go above and beyond with everything you do to the point where your doubters cannot even comprehend the massive action you are taking within your new work ethic.

Remember the story about Sylvester Stallone? During his speech at the Oscars after he captured his award for *Rocky* he read off all the negative things that each agency told him about his script as well as the idea of himself playing the actor of Rocky. Talk about the ultimate revenge. No matter what your goal is you WILL achieve it by putting in the necessary work and after you do I want you to take a bit to give yourself props. You deserve to be proud of what you have accomplished for you are progressing in the right direction of developing the best version of you that exists. Don't forget the work to be great doesn't stop when we have successfully completed our mission. It is time for bigger goals and that means more blood, sweat, and tears to fall from our bodies leading to even more rewarding accomplishments.

The people who look up to you are proud of your actions so there is no stopping now. At the same time, those same people looking up at you are putting in the extra work gunning for what you have. The grind must go on. Show them the way. For myself, nothing is more rewarding than when others seek out my help and advice by asking to pick my brain. I am now giving to others what was given to me by the many great men and women before me and by the people I look up to today. By passing your knowledge onto others you help keep the cycle of positivity and greatness to continue. The world is a much better place filled with happy positive people versus the negative critics who aim to drag anyone they can down to their level.

No matter how big or small our goals may be it is important to get them out there to be known. What this means is to tell people whom you trust what your goals are. Telling someone, like writing down our goals, makes us become more accountable. It is fuel to ignite the fire we need to take massive action. We want to prove what we are capable of, not just to others, but more importantly prove our worth to ourselves. Telling the ones we trust will also give us someone to hold us accountable and give us a swift kick in the ass when they see or sense we are slacking on our effort. A true friend will call us out on our shit and won't let us give up. Accountability partners are an asset to goal making.

"Even if you're on the right track you'll get run over if you just sit there."

- Will Rogers -

The idea of writing a book on personal development has been something I have kicked around in my mind for years. However, it's a bit difficult to attempt to tell people how to become a better stronger person when you're letting your own self slowly deteriorate into nothing more than a space saver. The seed to reach out and inspire thousands had been planted the minute I made the decision I needed to change who I had become, but it still was nothing but a thought. Action needed to take place; no longer could I just sit there and wait for things to miraculously fall into my lap. Everything changed the day I gathered enough strength to take that first step. Ever since that moment I have never looked back and haven't stopped grindin'. All day, every day. There is no other option. Life is not a game where we can hit the reset button whenever we feel the need to. We are not allowed to go back three spaces like we just received a Chance card. This is all we get.

The motivation was picking up steam with each passing day as I literally began to see my body transform back into its former athletic build telling me everything was going to be okay. With my physical health increasing daily I could now focus my attention on my mental state of mind. This is where all of the reading and writing I had been enthralled in became so vital for my development. A month into my recovery I remember announcing in one of the groups during the second phase of rehab that I wanted to write a book. Now it was out there. Even though I had said it to a group of strangers who looked at me like I had ten heads, I was now accountable to that statement. Things progressed rather quickly with not only my writing, but also the clarity of my head. All the information on becoming successful, having a positive mind set, and being happy already was stored in the back of my head from all those books I had read a decade prior. The experiences I have lived through since were the icing on the cake giving me the confidence and drive to turn my writing into *Stop Thinking Like That.*

My goal was very clear; to pour my heart and soul into doing whatever it took to make this book become a reality. And you know what? That is precisely what I did! No matter the outcome afterward, whether it becomes a New York Times Bestseller or I end up with a bunch of boxes collecting dust in my basement, I was not going to stop until the last page was written. My writing has been instrumental in my recovery. There is no recovery if I am not writing and there is no writing if I am not sober. The best part about it all is that I absolutely LOVE to write. I carry that pad of paper and pen with me at all times during the day because I never know what thought my come to my mind that will help me in the process.

The process consists of myself getting stronger mentally, physically, emotionally, and spiritually with each passing day. The process also includes putting every ounce of my being into helping others who need that push in the behind to get up and get going. To those struggling in life, whether with drug usage, a break-up, a death, a job loss, your savings drained due to a gambling addiction, whatever the case it may be, I want you to know that everything is going to be okay. If I can do it so can you. Just six months ago I was digging through people's garbage at night to collect cans to redeem assuring me I would not go thirsty the next morning. My life is indescribable in comparison to those days. That is all the hope you need to believe that you also can manage to get out of whatever funk you may be in at the moment. Just keep grindin'.

I have faced many critics on this mission and received countless sarcastic "Oh that's great Jason!"s followed by a roll of the eyes. I keep reminding myself that other's opinions have no relevance on achieving my objective, and I press on writing away while continuously filling my mind with more inspiration and motivation. I know that one day soon someone out there is going to be sitting in my shoes seeking out a story of hope and inspiration. That is all the motivation I would need but adding in the eye-rollers makes it that much easier to grind on.

With my goal crystal clear it was time to take massive action. My next step was writing my goal down so I could literally see it every day. My overall goal has not changed; it is to inspire thousands of people from all corners of the globe letting them know they can overcome anything they want to with the right mindset and the willingness to work. Writing *Stop Thinking Like That* is the culmination of how I pulled myself from the depths of desperation.

With a clear objective, I broke the overall goal down according to specific time frames of completion dates. As I taught you earlier about goal setting, I broke my goals down into small manageable chunks. I began with my immediate daily goals, then monthly, and finally pushed my goals out to one, five, and ten years. Sound familiar? Because it should. I was finally adhering to my step father's advice from a decade earlier. Better late than never, right? These goals are on a 5x7 piece of paper and taped on my night stand. They are the first thing I see when I wake up each morning and the last thing I see before I close my eyes at night. It has also been suggested to keep a copy of your goals on you at all times, whether in a wallet or purse. The constant reminder keeps the brain positive and having them handy keeps us on our toes at all times. We can always open up that piece of paper to remind ourselves of what we can do today to get closer to the final objective. Have you written your goals down yet? If not, take the time right now to write them in the blank space below.

____

____

____

____

____

Play Ball

Once I got the ball rolling it was Game On. Putting in long hours at the library became the norm every single opportunity I could get. Fortunately for me, the conviviality of the staff here at the Newburyport Public Library has been a welcoming sight each day as I proceeded up the lobby stairs and nestled into my chair in the computer section. I am very grateful for them putting up with me coming in and out multiple times a day.

I began writing *Stop Thinking Like That* while living with sixteen to eighteen other men in a recovery program house. Let me repeat that. My journaling evolved into *Stop Thinking Like That* while living with sixteen to eighteen other men in a recovery program house. Part of the rules in this strict house is that you cannot have a cell phone or a car until you graduate from the program six months after you first walk into the front door. I will be the first to tell you that it is extremely difficult to live a normal everyday life without two of the most important things used in today's society.

How did I get around you ask? I was huffing to and from the library and anywhere else I needed to go for that matter every single day, snow, rain, or shine, on my Diamondback bicycle or by putting one foot in front of the other. (Thank you to the ex who bought that bike for me while we worked together at Dick's Sporting Goods; much appreciated!) Whatever it takes! Thankfully it wasn't uphill both ways or I might not be talking with you right now. We only had access to the computer lab in our house on Tuesdays, so I would have to wait until then to print up any sections of *Stop Thinking Like That* that I needed to edit because the library charges $.15 per page and without a job money was tight. Oh yeah, the last two of the big four rules were no working and no intimate relations with females. All our focus was to be on our recovery and I will be forever grateful for that house and those rules. That last one was crucial for reasons I will discuss in a chapter further on.

With little to no distractions I could focus all my attention on becoming a healthier better person and I am achieving that slowly but surely through many things, near the top of which is writing this book. At night I would do the majority of my editing on the printed copies I had with a classic Bic pen. I found that it is extremely easier to edit with pen and paper versus attempting to on a computer with pop-ups, notifications, and such appearing every five minutes. Finally, after I finished editing I capped my night off with a couple of chapters from whichever book I was reading at the moment.

I know it must sound ludicrous to think that the majority of this book was written on a public computer at the local library that I hustled and bustled to by bike or foot every day from the recovery home I was living at with over a dozen other men. What the mind can conceive and believe, the mind can achieve. I hope you didn't doubt me when I told you I was NOT taking NO for an answer. I could have used every excuse in the book to quit writing when the times got tough or if I listened to the endless amounts of bullshit from the people who didn't have faith in me. I easily could have said "I can't!" but you all are worth every ounce of ink in this pen and every touch of the keyboard that has made *Stop Thinking Like That.* What those people didn't know was that I am powerful beyond measure and that I had already been through hell and back. The only way I could back up everything that I have told you thus far is by giving you a real-live glimpse into what it takes to overcome any obstacle to achieve your goals. Anything is possible if you truly want it to be. So, I ask you again, how bad do you want it?

[8]

Do as I Say Not as I Did

"It is hard to understand addiction unless you have experienced it."

- Ken Hensley -

Okay, let's finally have a chat about the elephant in the room; how the addiction to wanting more took a python hold of my life. Usually a person hits rock bottom before they find hope, but when did my bottom occur? There were too many an occasion where I felt I had reached the nadir of my sufferings. It could have been during pancreatitis bout number two of seven when, after viewing my MRI results, the doctor told me he would need to call my mother to tell her that her son was going to die due to his alcoholism. Or how about the numerous nights I spent driving around with Beanie filling up the back of my Jeep with empty cans I found from scouring through others' trash to be able to afford some liquor the following morning? Maybe it was the Christmas night my girlfriend found thousands of dollars' worth of Oxycontin? Merry Christmas, honey! I like to think it was the countless nights that I spent uncontrollably sobbing, begging the Man upstairs to please end the nightmare, yet when I awoke I found myself waiting at the 'packie' for the doors to open at 8am. But the real bottom for me was when my mother explained to me how she was told by her best friend to start preparing for my death because it was inevitable. My poor mom was prepping for her life without her only child. Can it get any more awful than that? I was completely naive and quixotic to think I had control of my life anymore. Drugs and alcohol were in complete control filling me with indignation for life. Unfair was an understatement, but it was all by my own doings.

All my addictions played a significant part in my time spent with the devil himself, but alcohol is what ultimately brought me to my knees. The problems started early and often as evident from the dismissal from my college's baseball team months after helping lead us to the national championship game. Fortunately for me, I left one powerhouse baseball program in Florida for one powerhouse baseball program in California. A change of coasts did not make a difference as alcohol was running the show and soon had a new

P.I.C. (partner in crime) in cocaine. I somehow managed to graduate with a Bachelor of the Arts in Criminal Justice degree on the five-and-a-half-year program. Ironic, huh?

I moved back to Florida shortly after graduating and found myself sitting in an office for a well-respected mortgage company. Hmm, is that an oxymoron? That employer became my longest tenured job in my life at exactly two years. With the money flowing in the partying hit new levels of extreme and occurred much more often. Soon I began to bounce from job to job and girlfriend to girlfriend. I was extremely codependent on both girlfriends and alcohol, but only the women in my life would be left high and dry. I will soon divulge into how to ruin a relationship. Stay tuned.

I eventually would lose interest with whatever job I was working at the time or became paranoid that my employer was becoming increasingly aware of my not-so-inconspicuous Houdini disappearing acts in and out of the office. At the end of the day, I managed to purposely get laid off, so that I could collect a weekly unemployment check. Stay classy, Jason.

Public Service Announcement: The author of this book is a trained professional, do NOT try this at home!

In the midst of all this chaos that I called my 20's I did manage to build two start-up businesses on my own, one of which I will elaborate in great detail further along in our journey. I also was fortunate to have played two years of professional baseball in the southwestern part of the country. The paychecks might have been miniscule, but it was pro ball nonetheless. As you may have guessed, neither of those endeavors were very successful by playing second fiddle to whichever addiction I was currently engaged in.

It is when I had managed to make it into my 30's that the heavy duty lifting of drinking and drugging would ultimately take over indefinitely. A handful of jobs, a few more girlfriends, those aforementioned seven extended stays in the hospital for bouts of pancreatitis (I also developed the beginning stages of chronic heart failure, a-fib, and pneumonia.), and one father dying on Christmas morning 2016 before my very own eyes due to the disease of alcoholism later, and I still pressed on in the cynical life of insanity. Like I said, I am not a quitter. That was until that sunny July afternoon when divine intervention took place ending over a decade long rollercoaster ride that I called life.

My life, for some odd reason, was spared. It took me a few months to figure out why God had saved me, but when I did I finally realized I was kept alive to save you from the gloom and doom life I had just occupied. Here we are riding out this journey together to help get us to where we want to be, and then we can pass it along to those in need, too. We are no longer fearful people, we are believers. We can. We will.

"Each night, when I go to sleep, I die.

And the next morning, when I wake up, I am reborn."

- Mahatma Gandhi -

My previous attempts at ending the nightmare that I called my reality were futile at best. It wasn't that I did not accept the fact that I was an alcoholic and an addict, but of more importance what I also accepted was that I wasn't strong-willed enough to think that I was capable of stopping. I would appease many a girlfriend and family member by preaching that my drinking days were behind me. And I meant those words every single time they announced themselves from my mouth, but my words were no match for the power that addiction bares. We are completely at the mercy of our addictions no matter the substance or action. It is in control, we are not.

To this day, I am still very much in awe that I am even sitting here writing to you. For anyone who has fallen victim to a life battling any of the hordes of addictions, or dealt with the loss of a loved one, or any other traumatic event that has/had taken over your life, the thought of finding inner peace and happiness is as farfetched as holding the winning Powerball numbers. It is truly a miracle that I am able to be discussing the fact that I have begun to find bits and pieces of the aforementioned inner peace and happiness in my life today. The fortunate events I have been blessed to experience are further proof that YOU, too, can achieve the inconceivable, no matter how deep into the black abyss you feel you've sunk. You no longer will be a prisoner of loneliness fearful that you received a sentence of life without the possibility of parole. This, too, will pass.

Once the blinds opened ever so slightly to allow a ray of sunshine to seep into my line of vision I knew I had found hope at last...or it had found me. From that point on there would be no limit to the extent I would go to not only emerge from those desperate times, but to flourish in the new life I had been so graciously gifted. I soon had a deep-rooted conviction that absolutely anything was/is possible and I was/am eager to go to any lengths necessary to share this powerful notion with anyone willing to listen. And I want to say thank you for allowing me the privilege to share my vision of hope and inspiration with you. Thank you for listening. Now, like I mentioned a few paragraphs prior, all I ask of you is to pass along these powerful words of motivation and inspiration, of love and joy, of strength and hope, to those in need, so they can join us on this beautiful journey. A successful life full of greatness and happiness awaits all those that commit to just keep grindin'.

Today I know I am doing exactly what I was put on this earth to do. I know that my purpose is much greater than my personal journey in recovery. I know my voice goes far beyond the ears of my friends and family who have to put up with me speaking incessantly about this newfound passion in my life. I know all of this is precisely what I am meant to be doing because I get the same tingly feeling throughout my entire body writing this book and speaking in front of audiences big and small about dealing with *life* as when I stepped up to the plate in the National Championship game back in 2003. In each situation there was and is nothing to fear. I know I am exactly where I am supposed to be, and I could not be happier!

I am committed to making my passion for bringing hope and inspiration to the thousands of people who are struggling to find a purpose and meaning in their lives, just like you and I were, my full-time profession. Nobody nor anything will get in the way of me fulfilling that commitment. I have made the pledge to do everything I can to execute the necessary actions to accomplishing this feat. I feel such a strong burn and urgency each morning when I wake that keeps pushing me further on in this journey, no matter what it takes, against all the odds, kicking and screaming, grinding every step of the way. I **will** help you. I **will not** be defeated. My eyes have that laser focus on the ultimate prize and yours need to do the same.

The passion I have for writing and sharing this book, for the opportunity to help others is what propels me every day to bundle up in multiple layers and hop on my bike or trek through the snow to the library to continue in the process while the rest of the men in the house are napping or sitting around playing cards. No disrespect to them, but I am here for a reason and that reason is to better myself for life moving forward and chase after greatness. I strive to have the best life possible for not only myself, but also for you. And if that means walking on iced covered sidewalks in -13 degrees wind-chill then that is what I am going to do. Nothing is going to stop me, not even the all-powerful Mother Nature. To get to where you need to go, to where others fear, you must be willing to do what they refuse to do. Now is the time to separate yourself from the rest of the pack.

I knew as I continued to get deeper into my recovery, slowly building up my mind, body, and soul to an optimal level that my reach would continue to grow. I gained more confidence in what I was doing in my attempts to inspire and give hope. The healthier I have gotten the more my confidence in my ability to help others has increased. No longer am I suffering from my habitual negativity. No longer am I suffering from the attachment I had to people, places, and things that restricted my growth. When we release ourselves from the reliance on the things holding us back from reaching our greatest potential we no longer are in fear of a life without them. We can now strive freely and openly to whatever *our* vision may be. It is our vision, no one else's!

It is 5:45 in the morning as my eyes crack open from yet another dreamless night. The sounds of smooth jazz playing from the TV still fills the parlor as I slowly begin to rise. I have zero chance of falling asleep naturally anymore so I go back to ole' faithful; jazz music. My mother would play Kenny G to put me to sleep as a child and thankfully he still does the trick for me during my adult child days, along with whatever sleeping pills I am prescribed at the given moment. Oh, I almost forgot the half empty warm alcoholic beverage that is left sitting on the coffee table alongside a few empty nips and a small plate. How could I ever try to fall asleep without that delectable concoction? That is the bare minimum needed to help put at ease a mind racing like the Daytona 500 from the dozen or so pain killers I consumed throughout the day. I just wish it could be like the old booze filled nights when I would just pass out like any normal person who drank too much that evening. But my mind, body, and soul are far beyond any amount of alcohol to cause such an achievement. Those nights of passing out are farfetched dreams these days, that is if I ever did dream. Spoiler alert; I don't, remember?

My excessively shaking hand finds the clicker and instinctively changes the tunes from saxophones to the talking heads on Sportscenter. The dark room lightens up from the new channel and lucky me, I notice one of the nips isn't empty after all and I remove the red cap and guzzle down the remainder. Even in the early dawn hours the rush of warm cinnamon whiskey into my body completely unphases my uber-tolerant throat. The foggy haze that is my mind clears up just enough to get me off the couch so I can put that warm half empty malt beverage into the freezer. I still have around two hours to get through until the packies open so every ounce counts until then. These shakes must be tended to somehow, right?

On my way back to the comfy sleeping habitat I call my couch I alter my route to where a normal person sleeps; the bedroom. I know there is half a pill left from the prior days exploits carefully hidden in my "medicine" drawer. Its concealment is in case someone burglarizes my house in the middle of the night and artfully sneaks past my two massive dogs, I still know it's in a safe place. I rescue the broken pill and soon have it crushed into a fine blue powder on the coffee table back in the parlor. As the said massive dogs lie on both sides of me, oblivious to my actions, I breakthrough my congested nasal cavity and a slight euphoria fills my brain. Ahh, normalcy! I lay back down between my dogs into my sunken crevice of the couch staring through the TV screen playing highlights from the prior nights' sporting events. The sun begins to slowly shine through the plethora of windows in the adjacent room as the countdown to eight am continues. Tick tock.

With the eight o'clock hour fast approaching I put on the everyday attire of an alcoholic; sweatpants and a hoodie. Fortunately for me I have enough hooded sweatshirts to keep a baseball squad warm, so the locals can't tell how disheveled I truly am when I venture out into public. My pups are now up and ready for their morning excursion down the stairs and into their grassless abyss I call my backyard. One day I will turn it into a luscious oasis for them to roam, I keep telling them and myself. But it's 7:57AM so I must tend to Jason's needs as their puppy eyes watch my Jeep speed off into the distance. A half mile later I arrive at my destination, stop number one of many for the day. Once I enter the store the owner acknowledges my entrance meaning its 8AM on the dot and he turns the cooler lights on. He knows my routine better than I do and has the change ready for my usual; a malt beverage, the local paper, and the daily numbers ticket for my nana. After we exchange pleasantries I head out with the mutual understanding of seeing one another in 24 hours.

Once home, my eager dogs patiently wait at the gate, tails wagging excessively as if I just got back from a long vacation. It is 8:05am. I first walk into my nana's first floor dwelling to hand her the paper and ticket in which she gives me three dollar bills even though I insist she don't every single morning. I head upstairs to pour my pups their morning meal and before they can indulge in some fine dollar store dog food I am already back to my crevice wetting my pallet with a delicious fruit punch flavored malt beverage. All inhabitants are now happy.

---

[9]

Old Ways Won't Open New Doors

"We all must suffer from one of two pains; the pain of discipline or the pain of regret. The difference is discipline weighs ounces while regret weighs tons."

- Jim Rohn -

One of the most important lessons I have learned in life is that you cannot succeed by sitting on the bench. How can we expect to get any better, physically, mentally, emotionally, or spiritually by being a spectator? Greatness is inside all of us, we just need to do the work to find it. When I would see others around me achieving success, smiling, laughing, and being overall joyful I needed to know how they did it. I was sick and tired of riding the pine and not enjoying what life had to offer me. I knew I **must** change my ways in order to change my life. Once I finally got up off my couch I threw myself into the fire, ready to do whatever it took to revive my life and find the happiness that I knew I deserved. I did not care what I had to do, I just knew I was willing to do it.

The next thing I know I was walking through the doors of a rehabilitation facility with open arms. I said to myself that I would do whatever I was told, whatever was needed of me, no matter how difficult it may be, or how much pain it may cause. Pain is temporary, and I knew that it was a necessary part of growth. I had already faced the worst pain life could throw at me with the never-ending vicious cycle I was battling in addiction. Whatever challenges you are going through you can and you will overcome. Massive action is the cure-all to all of our fears. And it is time for you to take action. No pain, no gain. Right?

The first major hit to my heart was walking away from my two beautiful dogs, Beanie and Shaq; my kiddos as I call them. I do not have any human children, but these two are as part of me like any person ever could be. They mean absolutely everything to me and my stomach ached and my heart hurt abandoning them by going off to an unknown distant land indefinitely. My eyes are tearing up as I type this because our pets are so innocent and full of so much love that they do not ever deserve to be anything but feeling love back by their owners.

For all of you pet owners, you know exactly what I am talking about. Our pets will never leave our side, no matter what our mood is they are right there loving us unconditionally. Every night Beanie and Shaq would snuggle up that much closer to their dad, consoling him as he cried uncontrollably begging for the nightmare to please stop. I knew if I wanted to give them the life they deserved I needed to get the necessary help to prevent the tears from flowing any longer. Beanie and Shaq were never able to get out and enjoy the world because they laid by their dad's side day and night while he withered away on the couch. Their father needed to get his mojo back and that is exactly what he set out to do!

To enjoy good health, to bring true happiness to one's family, to bring peace to all, one must first discipline and control one's own mind. If a man can control his mind he can find the way to Enlightenment, and all wisdom and virtue will naturally come to him."

- Buddha -

The attitude I had upon taking that first step in my recovery was something my mother taught me as a child. She would always remind me that "You can do anything that you put your mind to" and I was about to put that statement to the test. My mind was set on becoming the man I knew I was meant to be, inspiring and helping others on a daily basis, being a role model for today's youth, and simply making my selfless mother proud.

I read the Acceptance Prayer every morning and the final verse truly is life changing if we *accept* it: "I need to concentrate not so much as what needs to be changed in the world, but what needs to be changed in me and my attitude." Our attitudes can strongly restrict us from the progression in life we are striving toward. A bad attitude can anchor us down and keep us feeling like we are tirelessly swimming against the current. I am no Michael Phelps, so an attitude adjustment was exactly what was necessary if I wanted to change. We put in all this effort searching for answers for why our life is in shambles when all that is needed is a look into our own attitude. An attitude adjustment is well worth the positive results it can bring into our lives.

It does not matter if you are battling an addiction, going through a messy divorce or dealing with the death of a loved one, no matter the challenge you are facing we all must take the same road to redemption, to overcome the odds and find our true happiness again. The dynamics of how we got to our breaking point may be different, but taking the initiative is the first step in putting the pieces back together for us all. When moving on from great hardship you are going to experience hurt, there is no denying that. However, the hurt we feel is part of the healing that is necessary for us to move on. We must remember that sulking and blaming the world for our misfortunes will not bring back that which we have lost. Life goes on, whether you are ready to or not.

Here is a handkerchief to wipe away those tears and it is time to change your ways. First and foremost, we must want to change, to better the life we live, for *ourselves.* A lot of people may look at our desire to focus on ourselves as selfish, but in reality, this is as selfless of an act we can possibly take. I knew that in order for me to be the son that my mother deserved, the brother my siblings yearned for, a loving faithful boyfriend, the best co-worker, friend and of course, daddy to my pups, then I needed to fix me. Otherwise I would just continue to be cheating them of the man they had come to know and love over the years. I would continue cheating myself. It is time for you to be selfish and become the man or woman you know you are capable of being. By finding that loving, happy, driven person inside of you, you will be more apt to help others and find that you are good company to be around. I was about as helpful as a waterproof towel when I was completely occupied in my selfish activities. My company was not wanted by any of my real friends (not my bar buddies) nor did my family want me around. To be wanted again I needed to prove my worth.

We cannot have a pugnacious attitude toward change. The addicts, the lazy, the scapegoats, all have a proven track record that shows we cannot win that battle. Our way clearly hasn't worked as evident of us being here on this journey together attempting to pick up the pieces and make something of our lives. Our expectations can never exceed our effort so always be prepared to go all out in your effort if you want real change to transpire. Maximum effort yields maximum results. The work to be the best person you can will be ongoing and everlasting. When the work never ends the growth is limitless. We are going to grind our way into unknown territory to tap into our true potential.

If you want to change then you must be willing to break through the old limitations that have been holding you back. For the breakthrough to occur you must adopt and administer new empowering beliefs into your everyday life. A new mindset with these empowering beliefs allow for maximum growth no longer limiting your potential. There are no more excuses to be made once you implement these new beliefs, eliminating the negativity that once consumed your mind once and for all.

I know what it feels like when all the chips seem to be stacked up against you. The ubiquitous negativity feathering both sides of every single road we look down. It is inescapable and gobbles us up whole, spitting us out, until we are left with nothing but a skeleton of ourselves. I was once a completely broken individual, full of hopelessness and total despair. The despair had sucked the living life out of me, taking away any possibility of motivation that may have arose. There was no scientific formula or magical potion available for me to penetrate the broad wall of desperation. I needed to change. If I did not change then life was going to wipe its hands with me. I knew that I *must* make a commitment to myself to do whatever it took to fulfill my destiny of finding peace and prosperity in life. So, I took that first step en route to my new life. With no expectations other than willingly stepping forward and allowing myself to be vulnerable I had nothing to lose and everything to gain. Are you ready to commit to yourself and go after the life you want? Good answer, now let's continue the march to greatness!

"Success is your duty, obligation, and responsibility."

- Grant Cardone -

Who is it that you want to be? It is pretty clear that you aren't who you always envisioned yourself being nor are you living the life you've always desired or you wouldn't be reading this book right now. But here we are on this expedition together both chasing the lives we know we deserve, but that we must earn. You need to become committed to that person you desire to be. Desire is the key ingredient in the Law of Attraction, which we know as the "secret". The secret to living a fulfilling life is by putting our energy into the things we desire by looking within and deliberately using our thoughts and feelings. The more our mind sees and thinks about our innermost desires the more we are building up the momentum necessary to reach and attain them. It is a full-time commitment, absolutely nothing is handed to us.

All I can envision every single waking moment of my life today is becoming the best Jason Hyland I can possibly be in order to help as many men and women as I can. I have such a clear vision of myself standing on a stage looking out to thousands, sharing my life experience of depression, courage, strength, and hope. I know exactly the slacks and shirt combo I will be wearing as I enthusiastically speak words of encouragement to the energized crowd. No tie necessary. I envision myself sitting inside a Barnes & Noble in Dallas, Texas for a meet and greet with the people who I desire to inspire. I envision going back to the university where I was kicked off the baseball team months after being named the College World Series MVP (They have gone on to win three National Championships since our title game loss in 2003.) to share my testimony with the entire athletic department. I am beyond committed to doing whatever it takes to make these visions become reality. There is no other option because I unconditionally believe everything I have mentioned above is going to occur. Backing our beliefs with conviction forms an unstoppable force that will crush anything within its path.

I want you to pledge to go all-in on this commitment to your new life. There is no one foot in, one foot out. With a wishy-washy mentality you will only be setting yourself up for failure. This type of attitude leads us to running away with our tail tucked between our legs at the first sign of adversity. Think about it. When have you truly gone after something halfheartedly and accomplished the feat you set out to? If you have then it clearly wasn't something with much meaning behind it or your half-assed effort wouldn't have succeeded.

This approach to life is not going to make you a better stronger individual for future duties. And that is my goal each morning when my internal alarm clock starts buzzing. Today an actual alarm clock isn't necessary for me. My passion is what wakes me up every morning and that passion is to become a better stronger person today than I was yesterday. What is the point of even bothering to get out of bed if we don't desire bettering ourselves? To becoming a better son, daughter, husband, wife, father, or mother? I could go on infinitely. This takes us back to waking up excited for the day ahead, grateful that the opportunity for life is freely given to us. It is hard to attack our day with gusto if we are complaining before our head ever lifts off of the pillow. Are you truly committing to become the person you say you want to be if you're fighting the snooze button all morning? You will never achieve the best version of yourself if you continue on in your same old ways. Tactics must change for growth to occur.

I knew if I were to ever lift myself up out of my increasingly depressive state and strive for the life I had longed for then I would have to change my ways. I would have to take massive action to change everything about the person I had become in order to live the rest of my life as the man I knew I was meant to be. The man that is writing this sentence right now is an absolute far cry from the broken weak boy that did nothing more than exist a mere six months ago. I am not that boy anymore because I went all-in on my commitment to becoming the man that I had desired to be. It is your turn to join me and find out how great you can really be.

We have discussed a multitude of success stories by individuals who went above and beyond to get to where they wanted to go. Michael Jordan did not wake up one day to become forever known as the greatest basketball player that ever lived. Joe Manganiello worked tirelessly to hone his acting ability before he became the star of *True Blood.* Before Tony Robbins was the highly successful and most sought after public speaker in the world he was living in a barren studio trying to find purpose in life. The common theme for each of these individuals and the endless list of the greats of our time is they all were fully committed to making the required changes in themselves to reach into their untapped potential. They knew that if they were going to succeed in their quests for greatness that their current ways of living must change.

Successful people use the challenges that come about in their lives as opportunities to sharpen their abilities for future use. What they also do not do is get consumed with the unnecessary garbage that is vomited from the mouths of those looking to bring them down or simply to make themselves feel better. We lose focus on our personal growth to fine-tune our abilities when we are performing to gain the approval of others. Any energy we exude for the sole purpose of earning the acknowledgement and attention of our peers only weakens our chance at self-betterment. Too often we lose a sense of self by putting a mask on to fit in and this facade strips us of any chance at growth. When we have that laser focus on our inner being versus losing our way in our attempts to satisfy everyone else's depictions of who *they* want us to be, only then will we allow ourselves the opportunity to reach our full potential.

This all circles back to fear. The fear of success acts as a permanent blockade on our journey ultimately causing us to settle. It is often said that the greatest ideas lie buried in cemetery soil. Why? Because for every MJ, TB12, and Edison, there are a litany of people too scared to go after their dreams. Marianne Williamson's quote about fear directly resonates with all those who have taken their unlimited potential with them upon departing this earth. Why is our greatest fear that we are powerful beyond measure? I believe it is because we are scared of the work necessary to be great which leads to a life lived in mediocrity. We feel that with the more success we garner comes along more responsibility that we must bear and to many that is a scary concept. But, like I've said from the beginning, if we want to portray the best version of ourselves then there must be blood, sweat, and tears oozing out of us on a daily basis. With hard work comes great opportunity. I know for myself I am forever going to be seeking out who the best ME there is and if that means a lot of mountains to climb and rivers to cross, then I am excitedly willing to endure and conquer those obstacles for in my eyes that equates to happiness. It is time for you to join me.

[10]

Don't Cry Over Spilled Milk

"The only thing that comes to a sleeping man is dreams."

- Tupac Shukar -

One of my lifelong dreams has always been to open my own fitness training facility. This dream literally started as an actual dream that occurred one night back in the winter of 2011, a time that found me training rigorously for my upcoming season of pro ball. The vision I had in this dream was unlike any I had before, and it awoke me from a sound sleep around 4:00am. I immediately turned my bed lamp on and put pen to paper. I proceeded to draw out the blue print for the gym that I was just marveling at during my deep slumber and then I closed my eyes and drifted away. This was more than a dream, this was a subliminal message for what was to come.

After I hung up my spikes following the 2012 baseball season out in New Mexico I began a profession within the fitness industry. I found myself as a general manager for a personal training company, traveling back and forth between two gyms in the greater Boston area. I had a handful of trainers working for me at each location and I got to personally know every individual who wanted to sign up for our personal training. Engaging with people who have a desire for change is a very fulfilling process to be a part of. I would take the soon-to-be clients through an example workout, a trial per se, to get them accustomed to the type of exercises they would find themselves engaged in during their sessions. I may have only done the intake and chose the trainer I felt best suited their individual needs, but I still received unlimited satisfaction seeing how happy our clients were when they started to see the results of their hard work. Endless hugs became the norm as I saw lives literally transforming right in front of me.

I routinely drove through a college campus on my way to one of the clubs as part of my morning commute. As I was driving one day I noticed a "For Lease" sign on a building right smack dab in the middle of the campus that was formerly a paint distribution company. I stopped to take a look and it all hit me at once; this was the facility that would become the gym from my dream! It was nearly two years later, but my subconscious mind held onto my vision and never let go. I called the number on the window, set up a meeting with the landlord of the building, worked out the details, and before I knew it I was the proud owner of an empty paint facility! Conceived, believed, achieved!

I was well on my way to fulfilling that dream of opening a training facility, but the hard work hadn't even begun. After roughly two months of demolition, painting, organizing, too many Home Depot trips to count and lugging all the equipment over from my high school a few towns away (my school graciously donated the majority of the equipment), the dream had become a reality. Athlete's Performance Plus, or AP+, was now open for business. I had the name and logo already put together a couple years prior when I was running a boot camp, with the thought that maybe one day AP+ would become more than a group of women I instructed in an unoccupied office for a couple of hours a week. Speaking of that class, I absolutely loved my time with those women, filled with laughter and shaking our tooshes for the entire sixty minutes. The oldest member of our squad, in her mid-70s, would request Maroon 5's "Moves Like Jagger" to start off every session. I miss those ladies.

"Life is like a box of chocolates. You never know what you're gonna get."

- Forrest Gump -

There are three certainties in life: death, taxes, and countless failures. Kidding aside, let's focus on the latter. Failure is part of our everyday lives, no matter who we are, it does not discriminate. The successful individuals that we strive to emulate are the ones who use their failures to jumpstart their lives in a positive direction. Their failures motivate them to be great and they can do the same thing for you. Insecure people put their insecurities on you and you must flush them out. You must believe in one thing and one thing only: yourself.

I have always believed I was destined for greatness, I just took a very long round about detour after closing my facility down. During the opening months of AP+ my love for helping people unquestionably evolved as I began training my own clients and the list of clientele grew. As a former professional athlete, I know what it takes to get locked in to achieve greatness and now I was passing those traits and work ethics on to everyday people who walked through the doors. Like before when I saw my trainers' clients transform themselves into the person they sought out to be, I began seeing that occur first hand with my clients. Their daily grind produced results they never expected, but those are things that can happen in any aspect of life when you are willing to put in the work and take that first step.

Training others to help them achieve their ultimate selves was a blessing of which I was and still am very grateful for. I had truly achieved one of my life long dreams when I opened the doors to Athlete's Performance Plus. All the stars aligned just right for me along with a lot of dedication to the grind to get to that point, but I let it slip out of my hands at a slow rapid pace. This personal experience is proof that if we become complacent with the actions that have brought us beautiful things in life, they will be taken from us before our very own eyes. The loss of AP+ was yet another dream shattered directly correlating to my addictions.

I was committed to helping my clients achieve their personal goals, but little did they know I was completely lost on the inside. In the time that I had AP+ up and running I *never* once utilized MY gym for my personal well-being. The only actual working out that I engaged in was when I would demonstrate the exercise for a client, a feat that still mind boggles me to this day. Once I let my physical being slide I began to lose confidence in who I was. How could I tell people day in and day out how to transform their bodies when I was drinking in between sessions? When the confidence went, the motivation came to a halt and soon my life was spiraling out of control. If you ever feel that the activity you are engaged in is causing you to lose confidence and lowering your self-esteem then stop immediately. You do not want it to completely unravel your life before you know what hit you. I am telling you this because I do not want anyone to fall into a tailspin concoction consisting of isolation, alcohol, and depression like I did. I had become careless and undisciplined causing my routine to cease. Negativity soon followed and it was over for me. We will discuss ways to help alleviate our pain and sorry in the chapter about positivity.

"When life gives you lemons, don't make lemonade.

Give those lemons back and demand to speak

with life's manager!'

- Urban Dictionary -

It is very easy to get a case of the *f*ck its* when life smacks us in the mouth. We find ourselves saying "It was not my fault this, that, and the other happened to me." followed by "It was your fault, his fault, and definitely their fault!" Instead of playing the blame game, this is the time where we must begin to learn from our failures. Don Miguel Ruiz's *The Four Agreements* is a must-read inspirational book for the ages. The spiritual self-help book has become so popular that Patriots quarterback Tom Brady has been applying its principles to his daily life for over a decade.

Ruiz states that there are four agreements to living a life full of freedom:

- Be impeccable with your word
- Do not take things personally
- Do not make assumptions
- Always do your best in whatever you are doing.

By pointing the blame at everyone and everything but at ourselves, we are not being impeccable with our word. We must take responsibility for our actions, for our words, and stop being a willing participant in the blame game. By becoming impeccable with our word, we create positive energy and that starts with becoming honest with ourselves. By being honest with ourselves we allow others to see the integrity within our character make-up. If we are not honest with ourselves we certainly cannot be honest with others, similar to when we don't have confidence or love for ourselves, which we will delve into in more detail later. Our relationships and our life will be opened up to bigger and better opportunities when we begin to be honest with ourselves. Today is the day you stop blaming everyone around you for your struggles and you start to become impeccable with your word.

I very easily could have got a case of the *f*ck its* and pointed fingers all over for the demise of AP+. Instead, I accepted the responsibility that it was by my own doings that I had been knocked down by the failure of AP+, but I was not down for the count. We all make mistakes and fail, but remember, our greatest failures lead to our greatest successes. You may be hurting right now and have lost all hope due to something you have done or caused, but by no means does that mean life is over and you throw in the towel. You absolutely never give up! You are never alone, and I promise you that there is hope, for I, like thousands of millions of others, had thought I had finally done it and life was washing its hands with me. But boy was I ever wrong. You can. You will.

Losing my gym was 100% *my* fault, no questions asked. Instead of choosing to fall into a life of hopelessness, I needed to figure out what I needed to change to better prepare me for whatever life would have to offer in the future. It was my turn to overcome massive difficulties like Joe Manganiello did. We must realize that everything we have been through, no matter how great or how bad, someone else has been through that near exact situation before.

How we handle life's circumstances is what separates the failures from the successors. Accepting responsibility and being accountable for your actions is a major step in the right direction to avoiding future futility. By pointing fingers at everyone else and everything else we are delaying the inevitable wasting away precious time that could be used to progress toward our goals. Do not blame any other person or any other thing. I lost AP+ because of the choices I made, no one else's. Control that ego of yours, swallow your pride, and own up. Does it hurt? Sure. Will it take time to overcome? Maybe.

But let me ask you, what worth having in life does not require going through some pain and putting in a little bit of hard work? Remember, nothing is handed to us, unless your last name is Hilton or Kardashian, and we must continue to work to achieve that which we desire.

The ultimate motivator, former NFL all-pro linebacker Ray Lewis, states what it takes to get things done; "Effort is between you and you!" If you want something done only you can make that happen through hard work, discipline, and determination. The world is full of excuses and your pathway will always be littered with obstacles. But there is nothing that can stand up to the power of "I will!" The power at your command is truly awesome. "I will!" directs all that power. "I will!" takes you to positive places and brings you closer to the success you desire. Now tell yourself "I will make it happen. I will find a way. I know I can do it, and I will." Louder! Say it with such conviction that you feel it within you. I want you to feel the positivity burning inside your body the more you tell yourself "I will!" There are no more excuses and there is no one else to blame but yourself if you do not put in the effort necessary to succeed in all facets of your life. You can! You will!

Have I mentioned that failure is inevitable? I need to assure you get the point, so please do not get discouraged when it does happen. You cannot achieve success without failure as it's the gateway to opportunity. Self-proclaimed motivational king Elliot Hulse describes failure as "an experience that lends to wisdom that ultimately makes you a stronger version of yourself." It is okay to fail, you just need to pick yourself back up when you do, learn from it, and continue to press forward. Without the darkness in your life you would never be able to see the light. We are all a work in progress and we all will experience failure in our lives, time after time. The more we fail, the more opportunity for us to learn, the stronger we become.

The true failure in life is not trying at all. The real men and women say I failed, instead of what if. I don't know about you, but I certainly do not enjoy going through life playing the 'what if' card. If you want something go after it. Period. Constantly visualize whatever it is you want until it is thoroughly ingrained in your mind. From that point, it's up to you to take action and get up, dust yourself off, and continue the push until you reach your goal no matter what. Just keep grindin'.

If you don't go after what you want, you will never know what you are truly capable of. The sky is the limit for those who want it, not just for the esoteric overachievers. They believe they can and now it is *your* turn. Face your fears because behind that fear is the person that you yearn to be. Embrace the pain that failure causes you, remember the hurt you went through time and again. The pain and suffering will make achieving the ultimate success you've dreamt of much more rewarding. It will drive you until you get to the top of the mountain giving you a cause to celebrate. Be proud of yourself for the dedication to all your hard work and the self-discipline you have put in to reach the pinnacle of success has paid off. You have earned the satisfaction to smile. Once you are done basking in your well-deserved glory it is time to begin looking up for the next highest peak.

[11]

Procrastination Station

"To wait for someone else, or to expect someone else

To make my life richer, or fuller, or more satisfying,

Puts me in a constant state of suspension."

-Kathleen Tierney Andrus-

What are you waiting for? What is it that's holding you back from becoming the person you want to be? From living the life you want to live? Why are you procrastinating when time is not on your side? We are all guilty of being procrastinators at some point, but when it comes down to it, winners do not wait, they act. You will adopt a "take-no-prisoners" attitude from here on out. If you want something you will go out and get it! There is no better time than now because tomorrow is not guaranteed and never will be. As we discussed in the last chapter, it's a common theme to hear people speak about the *what ifs* of their lives. What if I leave the job I am unhappy working at and I don't find a new job? What if I end the relationship that I no longer want to be in, but I am unhappier than before? What if I ask her out and she says no? The grass may not always be greener on the other side, but *what if* you never know?

A great exercise I have learned during the process of recovering who I am is what I call the 'learn and burn'. There are many different versions of this exercise, but they all end the same: burning the letter which you have just written. I featured my letter at the very beginning of this book before the story even unfolds in *Stop Thinking Like That* because I wanted you, the reader, to realize that regardless of how tight the grip something may seem to have on you, you can unleash yourself from it. No matter the depths we have fallen, there will always be hope for us to find the strength and courage to pick ourselves up and dig ourselves out of that hole. It will not be easy, we will fall down more than we would like, but if we keep grindin' we will find ourselves looking down at the pit.

You have already begun your journey to recovering who you are and discovering the best you that exists by reading *Stop Thinking Like That* this far. Now is the time to put the clamps on what has been holding you back, holding you hostage from discovering the greatness within you. Use that handy Five-Star notebook and start jotting down the things that immediately come to mind when you think of what is in your way.

Today is the day you write that letter. Not tomorrow, not next week, but today. I want you to pour your heart, your tears, and all the emotions burrowed up inside of you onto that piece of paper, withholding absolutely nothing. What is it that is holding you back from greatness right now? What is it you fear that has kept you from moving forward? Are your friends, family, and loved ones talking you out of pursuing your dreams? From pursuing your passion? Is someone ripping your confidence right out from underneath you because they do not have confidence themselves? Why are you so scared of the word NO? Do not stop writing until there is nothing left to hold you hostage any longer. Your dreams are your dreams, no one else's! It is time to let go of all the negative people, places, things, and situations that do not want to see you succeed.

Go grab a lighter and find a safe place for it is time to burn all that outside noise restricting you from finding the greatness within. Light up that paper and watch as all the bullshit slowly disintegrates before your eyes. There no longer is anything that can hold you back from finding happiness, from achieving success, or from finding joy in life. There is nothing that you cannot overcome. The haters, the naysayers, the critics, the doubts, the insecurities, the endless negativity, all of that simply does not exist anymore for it is all sitting in front of you in a puddle of ash. Feel refreshed and rejuvenated? Great, now let's grind on further.

Greener Pastures

Why are we so fearful of the other side? I believe we tend to become content with where we are in our lives and settle. What do we settle for? Less! Living life in fear is a debilitating process. Fear is the number one thing that holds us back from greatness, disallowing us from ever seeing what we are truly capable of accomplishing in life. We think that the *Lifestyles of the Rich and Famous* is for members only handpicked by Robin Leach. Our mind is constantly being perpetrated by negative self-defeating thoughts like "No way can I ever have that house. I'll never be able to move out of this apartment. Those beautiful weddings on the beach only happen in soap operas and rom-coms. True romance can only be found watching Rachel and Ryan fall in love in *The Notebook*." Wake up call to everyone, but *The Notebook* is based on a true story! It is possible for ALL of us, rich or poor, young or old, male or female, black or white, to find true serenity in life. You are NOT inadequate, you truly are powerful beyond measure and it is up to you to seek out that power.

Fear is a natural stepping stone for us all. By living in a state of constant fear we are holding ourselves back. There is a whole world out there waiting to be found once we learn to overcome the fear barrier. There is no barrier too big or too strong for you to defeat.

Believing in yourself followed by taking that first step into the unknown is the start. When you find yourself standing at a crossroads in life, are you going to peek through and say "No way, I cannot do that!" or will you put one foot in front of the other and see what all the fuss is about? Start walking, now! And as you do you will notice all the mythical characters you only watched from afar on the big screen are right there next to you. They faced the same fears you and I did, but when they were met at the gates to opportunity by the gargoyles they pushed them aside with confidence, grit and determination. They did not take NO for an answer. Neither did Edison, Jordan, Brady, Manganiello, and the list goes on.

When we begin to stop fearing the unknown we open up those doors to opportunity. We can never achieve our true wants and desires if we don't push open the doors with conviction. You, me, and everyone else deserves the opportunity to live out the life we dream of, but as deserving as we may be, we still must go out and earn it. And that takes strength, fortitude, and overcoming our fears.

It is okay to be scared, but it is not okay to let that fear be the deciding factor for our personal growth. I want you to know that greatness is upon you, you just need to be willing to put in the work. You can do whatever you want without limitation. Whatever it is in life that you want you have. It is going to take an inordinate amount of work, you are going to have to push and push and push, and then when you hit the limit you are going to force yourself to push even further. Somebody right now is out there outworking you. They are failing, getting back up, and continuously pushing themselves. Someone right now is putting in that work. Are you going to let them outwork you and achieve *your* dreams?

Motivation does not exist when fear is present. We make decisions based on our feelings, instead of taking control of the moment due to fear. Go after the moment with the *Do It Now* mentality. You may not be motivated at the moment, not confident in who you are today, and do not have the courage to go after the life you desire. And that is okay because you can still push yourself forward if you *Do It Now*. Your mind and your heart know what you want to do, know what you want to have, and they will work through the feelings of doubt and insecurity you may have toward your desires. Those desires were planted there long before you got into the place you currently reside and your life flipped upside down. Maybe you are dealing with a breakup, job loss, currently in rehab, or you just simply want to live a better life. Your mind knows that and will subconsciously act to help you get there.

If It Is To Be It Is Up To Me

If this isn't the life you want to live then it is time to do something about it. There are going to be the days you need to break through all the bullshit and those days will come often. Bullshit exists all around you, but it does not determine where you are striving to go or who you are trying to be. Hike your pants up a little higher today because it starts now. If you want to change, then DO IT! Are you unhappy in your relationship? Do you despise going to work every day? Are you sick of what you see in the mirror? Well, what are you going to do about it? Things will not change if you do not take action and put in the work. Nothing changes if nothing changes.

Okay, so you are stuck in a dead-end job and cannot climb the financial ladder any further. Been there, done that. I couldn't tell you the amount of jobs I went through in the past decade, seemingly always getting bored of what the duties entailed and realized my paychecks had hit their ceiling. It is time to start using the good ole internet and search. There are dozens of job search engines, from Zip Recruiter to Career Builder that you can use to your advantage. Start getting your name out there and send an updated resume to multiple jobs that peek your interest. Then send your resume to more. Do not be shy, expose yourself to bigger audiences, and open yourself up to more opportunities. Find the job that you will wake up excited to go to, that makes you sing like you are vying to be the next American Idol as you drive down 95 (or I5 for you west coasters) in route to the office. If we are doing what we love, we will never work a day in our lives.

Maybe you are with the right employer, but you aren't seeing yourself moving up the promotional chain like your peers? Well, then it is time for you to take massive action because clearly what you are currently doing is not working. Are you using your time efficiently or spending half your day surfing the internet? You must separate yourself from the pack in order to stand out and make a positive name for yourself. Are you the first one in the office, turning on the lights and putting that first batch of coffee together? Or are you moseying on in at your leisure, carefree and careless?

I can tell you firsthand there is *always* someone watching you, regardless of your position at your company. Other employees see your misguided actions as a sign of weakness and they'll use it to their advantage to surpass you quicker than that fresh pot of coffee you should have been brewing. Management sees right through the bullshit and knows when they are better off without the lazy web-surfing salesman or woman who is forever stuck staring at the clock. Clock-watching is not a positive habit or trait for anyone trying to succeed in his or her given profession. That is separating yourself for all the wrong reasons. As Ben Affleck so elegantly enlightens us during his emphatic monologue in one of my all-time favorite movies *Boiler Room*; "You are required to work your f*cking ass off...A piker walks at the bell." If you want to be noticed, be noticed for your outstanding work ethic, your promptness to action, your resiliency, sufficiency, discipline, eagerness to learn, excellence in time-management, superior goal-setting ability, persistence, and fearlessness of being uncomfortable.

If you are unhappy with the person you are with then it is time to walk away. We cannot change people, only they can change themselves. It is not fair to either of you to continue with the irreparable stagnant life you are stuck in. Stop wasting your time and theirs and say goodbye. Remember this life is all we are blessed with and time is not on our side. Do not spend your life doing things you do not want to do with people you do not want to be with. Quit delaying the inevitable and face the fear of being alone. Not tomorrow, not next week, but right now! Yes, it is going to hurt initially and maybe for a little longer than you hoped, but you are doing both of y'all a favor by walking away before it is too late. Pain is temporary and it will pass. Aggravation and frustration day in and day out with your partner, however, will continue indefinitely if you don't make the proper decision and say goodbye.

I have made this mistake a few times and, in the end, I only caused more heartache for us both by staying in the relationship for the sake of my girlfriend's safety and protection. I was too scared to hurt her and breaking her heart, but wasn't I already doing that by my actions or lack thereof in the relationship anyways? Do you and your partner a favor by wishing him or her the best and walk away. We will take a more in-depth look at my love life and all that entails further along on our journey. Get your popcorn ready!

Sick of those love handles and all that extra flab hanging out under your arm? Then get off your ass and do something about it. Lack motivation? Set multiple alarms on your phone to remind you that your ass jiggles in ways it is not supposed to jiggle, put post-its all around your apartment with motivational quotes, read more motivational books like this, watch any of the thousands of inspiring and motivating videos on You-Tube, and throw away that damn scale! The number on a scale does not tell us if we are happy or not with what we see in the mirror. All it does is make us mad, upset, and demoralized so please do yourself a favor and pack it away with your Christmas decorations. Or better yet, sell it at your next yard sale. Just get rid of it this moment.

This isn't a solo mission so if you have the money then get yourself a personal trainer. I know we cannot do it all on our own, that we need that kick in the butt every now and then. A trainer will do that for you. He or she will be that reminder you desperately need. You certainly will not be happy with yourself at the end of the month if you just wasted $300 on a trainer you used once. A trainer is absolutely worth the investment for your health. Now unglue your body from the couch and put on your gym attire; the following chapter will be here waiting for you once you complete your workout. Don't forget your water bottle, hydration is a must. More on healthy eating in the pages to come when we get into nutrition.

[12]

The Paradox of Vulnerability

"Our deepest fear is not that we are inadequate. Our deepest fear is that we are powerful beyond measure!"

- Marianne Williamson -

He followed the trail of blood up the long hill through the new developments being built. His friend ahead of him somehow remained silent as he was sprinting like a cheetah chasing down his prey, while blood gushed profusely from his mouth. That boy bleeding was me after a horrific accident where I caught my four front teeth on the net of an adjustable basketball hoop. An oral surgeon was rushed into the emergency room to miraculously put my palate back together and flip those four upper teeth back to their original position since they were facing the sky when he walked in. The surgeon then attached a metal wire from the back of one side of my mouth around to the other like a horseshoe, in an attempt to hold my teeth together. Those four teeth have been dead since that accident and my crooked smile has become part of my character.

My silence was due to the fear of my father seeing me with tears running down my cheeks in complete agony. I couldn't cry and show weakness, despite the fact that my mouth looked like it went through a blender. Hyland's weren't allowed to cry and we certainly were too macho to ever be vulnerable. Vulnerability did not exist in our household.

I learned my lesson a year or two prior when I put my fist through my next-door neighbor's cellar window, beating a neighborhood friend to the punch. All seemed well as I puffed my chest out for winning the silly contest, but then I saw the blood. Blood must mean pain, so I thought, and I let out a loud cry, running right past my father standing in the driveway and into the house to my mother's aid. As she consoled me and wrapped my hand up my father walked in. I knew I was in trouble. Not for breaking our neighbor's window, of course, but for sobbing and showing pain. "What the fuck are you crying for?" he barked at me as my mom grabbed the keys. I ended up with nearly a dozen stitches, which I can still count on my right hand to this day. The art of stitching certainly has improved since that day nearly twenty years ago. But I am still a Hyland and weakness is not allowed in my vocabulary. Instead, ingrained in me is that I can never show vulnerability and let my feelings be known. All from that sunny summer day when I was just an innocent little eight-year-old.

Vulnerability is nearly always synonymous with weakness, but in reality, you cannot have one without the other. If you're vulnerable you're weak. If you're weak you're vulnerable. According to The American Heritage Dictionary, vulnerable is defined as "susceptible to physical injury or attack". Weakness, however, is defined as "the state of being weak or personal defect or failing." A person who is seen as weak "lacks physical strength, energy, or vigor, and is likely to fail under pressure or stress." Based on these definitions, being vulnerable, to me, means you're more prone to pain, suffering, and shame because of your weaknesses. Of course, I am not focusing on the physical pain when determining vulnerability. Our vulnerability is inside of us, eating away at our self-esteem and building up our ever-growing shame. All the hurt, guilt, and shame we are holding in is due to our fear of being vulnerable. It is not easy having the stigma of being vulnerable attached to you, especially for all of us big strong men. With all of this unnecessary rubbish being thrown around inside of us, what are we supposed to do?

There are many things we can and must do if we want to accept who we are, believe in ourselves, and allow ourselves to be vulnerable. Dr. Brené Brown wrote a fascinating book on vulnerability, *Daring Greatly* that was instrumental in helping me to learn acceptance during the early stages of my recovery. She states that if we want to reclaim the essential emotional part of our lives and reignite our passion and purpose, we must learn how to own and engage with our vulnerability and how to feel the emotions that come with it.

Life is vulnerable, ladies and gentlemen. People are going to have their opinions of you, good and bad, whether you like it or not, and you have little to no say in the matter. That is simply life. I have practiced living by the mantra of the *Serenity Prayer* for many years, well before I turned to abstaining from drugs and alcohol. If we can learn to "accept the things we cannot change" our lives will fill up with more potential and freedom. All we are in charge of is how we respond to other's behaviors, which means we are always in charge of our actions. Not them.

One of the great speeches in the history of our great country was by Teddy Roosevelt back in 1910 in Paris, France called *Citizenship in A Republic.* During the now famous excerpt known as "Man in the Arena" he powerfully delivers a message that has resonated with multiple generations since his epic speech over a century ago.

> **It is not the critic who counts; not the man who points out how the strong man stumbles, or where the doer of deeds could have done them better. The credit belongs to the man who is actually in the arena, whose face is marred by dust and sweat and blood; who strives valiantly; who errs, who comes short again and again, because there is no effort without error and shortcoming; but who does always actually strive to do the deeds; who knows great enthusiasms, the great devotions; who spends himself in a worthy cause; who at the best knows in the end the triumph of high achievement, and who at the worst, if he fails, at least fails while daring greatly, so that his place shall never be with those cold and timid souls who neither know victory nor defeat.**

Why should anything that anyone says about us even matter? They have no clue what we have lived through; they just live with their false pretenses and assumptions. No one has ever stepped foot into your arena nor have they a clue about the daily battles you are forged in. They are not the ones marred in dust and sweat and blood, battling *life*! Forget them! Don't ever stop in your quest for greatness; live life on your terms, shed those tears, face uncertainty head on, and know that YOU will succeed. You will get up off the ground, time after time, never giving up and never giving in. You can. You will.

Society has built this idea that vulnerability is a bad thing, when in all reality it is a necessary part of the growing process of human beings. To me, being vulnerable is an exceptionally strong and honorable characteristic for one to possess. It takes a great deal of courage to come out and express your vulnerability to the public as it is an acceptance of sorts. We are accepting our flaws, our defects, and owning up to our stories. We are admitting to our mistakes and that we do not have all the answers. When vulnerability can be damaging is when we hold all those aforementioned feelings of guilt, shame, and hurt inside of us. The more they fester and grow within us the more we fall into isolation from society because we fear the outcome of owning up to the circumstances we have created. We fear the past will define who we are, and we will be seen only by our defaults. We start to get a strong sense of unworthiness and our isolation only gets further entrenched into our everyday lives. What we need to do is become immune to other's opinions limiting our suffering. Everyone has their own belief system and there is no need to focus on anyone's other than our own.

Why is it not okay for us to show our real feelings? To show we care? To show tears? By becoming vulnerable we allow our true character to come out showing that we do not fear *fear*. That is what strength is. The man with the biggest ego is very rarely the strongest. The man who shows on the outside he is indestructible is usually one of the weakest inside. There is nothing wrong with either if they allow vulnerability into their life. The strongest men and women are the ones who accept who they are by owning up to their positives *and* negatives because we ALL are full of both.

Fearing inadequacy is the fear we have of the unknown, of the limitless ability we each possess. We must be willing to defeat adversity on a daily basis, conquering the stuck-up neighbor who looks down on us, the opinion of the in-law who wishes we never married their child, the co-worker always talking behind our back at the water cooler, and the friend who tells us to give up on our goals because we are not worthy of achieving such grandiose things. Adversity is not going to give you a call and tell you when it is going to visit you in life. There is no premeditation as adversity comes unannounced packing a punch. It may take blood, sweat, and tears to face the adversity, but that is what being vulnerable is all about.

Are you willing to go out of your comfort zone? To ask for help? To cry on another's shoulder? To simply say, "I don't know." When you are willing to do these things, you are allowing yourself to become vulnerable. You are willing to show you accept YOU! And that is when our potential becomes limitless. The knots in our stomach begin to slowly untwist, the gaping hole in our chest begins to fill with fresh air, and we begin to open the curtains that we have been too scared to see behind. The light has now broken through the darkness and we no longer see our goals in double vision. We start to believe we can do whatever we put our mind to, just like our mothers have always told us. The only person who can get in the way of our dreams, aspirations, and visions of joy is the person looking back at you every single day in the mirror. When we defeat the opinions of others and accept the person in the mirror, we are well on our way to living a limitless life, full of vulnerability, and courage, and worthiness. A limitless life is worth all the bumps and bruises and sleepless nights.

The Fear Factor

I have always had an extreme fear of both snakes and spiders. Most children seek out bugs and insects during their excursions into the forests, but not this kid. I distinctly remember playing in the woods between my house and the football field behind it as a child and I lifted a board up that was in the middle of a path. Much to my surprise there was an enormous snake slithering in my direction for waking her from her beauty sleep. I did not think anacondas existed in Massachusetts! Come to find out it was a foot-long harmless garter snake.

Fast forward to my freshman year in college in Florida when there was a petting zoo on campus from the local wildlife refuge. Of course, the zoo keepers had to bring along both a giant python and a tarantula. Here was my chance to face two of my fears head on. After much debate for what seemed like hours the keeper proceeded to place the mighty python around my neck like I was Britney Spears at the VMA's. I needed to have actual proof that I wasn't just dreaming so the keeper snapped a Polaroid of the snake and a smiling Jason. After I survived the near-death experience with the python it was time to take my last breath of life before the tarantula would take me down. There was no Polaroid this time, but I did hold the spider until it was drenched by my sweaty palm. Fortunately for me, life went on.

The above examples are minute when compared to the fears we face when trying to turn our life around or the fears we have during challenging times. But it is an example of having the faith that everything will be okay, and we can move ahead under any circumstances. If we cannot face the little fears we have daily, then we certainly are not ready to tackle the life-altering events that we fear. We need to allow fear into our lives and not fear, fear. It is just another obstacle on your way to the top and by taking massive action your fears are soon far back in the rearview mirror.

What is fear? I prefer to think of fear as our imagination allowing negativity to bounce around inside our mind causing expectations of a negative outcome or rejection. This is why fear restricts our vision and limits the possibilities for us to succeed. Remember, our potential is limitless if we have faith. For the addicts and alcoholics, we choose to numb ourselves with substances and recoil from any fear present in our lives. We cannot rise above the overwhelming feeling that the pain and suffering addiction brings so our solution is to continue in the vicious cycle. We are scared to stand up to our fears based on our previous failures.

Today failure is no longer going to distract us and hold us back. We have solutions that solve those problems now. Accepting fear is the step we now take because having awareness of our fears show that we are moving in the right direction. We are progressing toward new levels we have not yet achieved, to the uncomfortable, the unknown, and that is where *greatness* lies! Fear is not an excuse; it is a sign to continue pushing forward into those unknown areas. I want you to have faith and keep grindin'!

At the beginning of our journey I asked you to have *faith* in me and what I was about to tell you. What exactly is faith? To me, faith is what defeats fear. Sharon Salzberg wrote a fascinating book, simply titled *Faith,* about her life-changing trip to India where she was introduced to the Buddhist philosophy. After reading this book my perspective had completely changed when it came to fear. I could now grasp why we fear certain things and how we can triumph over them. I felt I now possessed the proper attitude and belief system necessary for when life challenges me. Salzburg describes faith as:

> **Suffering leads to faith. In times of great struggle, when there is nothing else to rely on and nowhere else to go, maybe it is the return to the moment that is an act of faith. From that point, openness to possibility can arise, willingness to see what will happen, patience, endeavor, strength and courage. Moment by moment we can find our way through.**

She further goes on to state that faith is "not a definition of reality, not a received answer, but an active, open state that makes us willing to explore." Facing our fears is our willingness to explore the unknown. When we have faith in what we are attempting to do or trying to accomplish fear is no longer obstructing our progress toward the life we want. Faith is the endless possibilities and opportunities that we spoke of earlier about possessing a positive mindset. At our darkest hours it is faith that allows the light to shine through. Faith gives us the hope that we can be the person we desire and live the life we always dreamed of. Without faith, there is no hope or possibility and fear has triumphed once again. Like I said from the start, I need you to have faith in what I am telling you and believe in the process of our journey together.

[13]

Along Came Paulie...Positive

"The positive thinker sees the invisible, feels the intangible, and achieves the impossible."

- Winston Churchill -

As I spoke of earlier, I begin each morning by writing out a list of that which I am grateful for. Of course, there are some repetitive items on this list, but I will be forever grateful for such things as family, warm clothes, food on the table, my kiddos, and simply waking up, let alone in a bed. I certainly am not the first to start my day off this way as it is a trait I have picked up from many of the successful individuals whom I respect, admire, and strive to emulate. The same individuals who are living a life full of happiness are living a life full of gratitude. Beginning your day by writing down the things you are grateful for puts you in a positive state of mind from the onset and paints the picture of a better world in your mind. Studies show that gratefulness will make you more productive at work and more successful in your relationships. Listing things you are grateful for forces the brain to focus on the positives and leaves no room for negative thoughts to enter. Start your day off on a positive note by writing down what you are grateful. If you want to dominate the day you must start them off by owning your mornings and that starts NOW! Keep grindin'.

Positive thinking is defined as the mental attitude in which you expect good and favorable results. There are many benefits of positive thinking, in particular promoting overall better health. According to the Mayo Clinic, positive thinking helps, among other things: to reduce blood pressure, to lower the risk of death due to cardiovascular disease, less risk of the common cold, reduces the rate of depression and stress levels, better mental health, better coping skills, more efficiency in managing stress and anxiety, and in increasing our life span. To be the best version of yourself you first must be the healthiest version and positive thinking plays a major role in doing so. I have been all aboard the power of positive thinking train for many years and when my life got derailed a major part of it was due to forming a negative belief system. Today I choose to kill that negativity and speak positivity into existence.

There are many questions around how one can simply become and remain positive when their life seems to be caving in all around them. These were the same questions I was receiving from many around me when I showed the confidence that the nightmare was over. Do not get me wrong, there is no doubting that life can straight up suck at times. No one is exempt from hurt nor is anyone immune to failure as I have clearly endured plenty throughout my lifetime. It is how we learn to respond to our trials and tribulations that shape our lives. We must remind ourselves that all things pass, and our experiences will always change, for better and worse. Are you going to choose to *grow* from the traumatic events in your life or are you going to simply go through the motions? Will the negative experiences in your life define who you are? Absolutely not!

Time to Train Your Brain

We can train our brain to think more optimistically and turn negative thoughts into positives with a little work and elbow grease. The first step is to stop focusing on the things you could have done better and turn your attention to what you have accomplished. Life is about progress, not perfection. The power of positive thinking begins with how we view and speak to ourselves. Do not say anything about yourself that you wouldn't say to anyone else. That is the golden rule and I suggest you start practicing it at this moment. Go ahead and say, "I am a great person!" right now before reading any further and do not ever forget those words. Practicing self-talk is something we can do anytime anywhere. A great time to rehearse is while you are driving so just bob your head around like your listening to the soundtrack of *Night at the Roxbury* and passersby will think you are jamming out. Little do they know you are en route to greatness

Knock knock. Who's there? A broken pencil. A broken pencil who? Never mind it's pointless. A horrific joke I know, but I bet you chuckled a little bit. Come on, don't lie. Laughter is another way to help turn a negative thought into a positive one. When times are tough search for the humor in the situation and do not be afraid to SMILE. The simple act of smiling has been scientifically proven to lift one's mood and due to a powerful chemical reaction, it can trick the brain into feeling a sense of happiness. Like I said before, turn that frown upside down! Our cell phones are filled with far more positive emojis than negative ones because you are meant to be happy. Trust me, I could only fake a smile or a mere smirk for years due to my insecurity about my large crooked upper front teeth due to that childhood injury. If I can smile today, you can too. I have faith in you.

A funny thing happened the day I walked into the detox facility last summer. I have always loved to read, as I have discussed prior, but one thing I never engaged in was writing. That changed on the first night of the day that forever changed my life. I started a journal simply titled "Detox" and on page one the headline was "Day 1". Original, I know. The next thing I know I was spewing out jargon I had no idea was tucked away deep inside me and the pen began to flow effortlessly. Each passing day my journal entries increased drastically. Now, here I sit writing to you about my life struggles and triumphs all the way on page 145.

Journaling has helped me through some of the most trying times of my life. All the hurt and suffering that was locked up inside me for years was filling up notebook after notebook (I am currently using four different ones right now. OCD to the extreme.) with each stroke of the pen. I was healing. The negative experiences and the traumatic events of my life unfolded onto paper, slowly allowing positivity to overtake them. Soon, I was writing down my dreams, aspirations, and a gratitude list, training my brain to scan for as many positives as possible. Not only was I writing about the power of a positive mind, I was speaking it, every day to anyone willing to listen. I am living proof of the magic that can occur by turning our mind into a machine full of positive thoughts.

I suggest you grab your keys and head to the local CVS to pick up a fresh pack of your favorite Bics along with a shiny five subject notebook. It is time to write so much your hand cramps up. Don't be shy holding nothing back. Pour your heart into your writing and you will feel the healing commence. Tears will undoubtedly start flowing down your cheeks with each drop representing a step closer to serenity. Of course, it is not supposed to be a breeze to get to the level of happiness you desire. Once my past, good, bad, or indifferent, was transcribed onto paper I began to slowly heal and learn information about myself I never knew existed. By pouring out all the guilt, pain, and shame that are tormenting you inside you are releasing the negative thoughts from your mind.

Your past will no longer hold you back as a bright future is ahead of you. In this moment continue to write without pause allowing yourself to be free. Write about past experiences of happiness, too, as a reminder of that feeling you are seeking. Give yourself the hope that you can and you will be happy once again. It is time to improve the new you making those experiences significantly better.

Another key way to helping turn our moods around is by exercising. If you are already a workout warrior, then kudos to you. For the rest of us, let's hit the pavement or the local fitness center. I was that workout warrior for many years, going to the max nearly every day, especially during my off-season training. People would stare at me during my workouts like I was some crazed beast. I did not care what others thought because I knew I was bettering myself with every repetition. Other's opinions will not help you become a healthier individual so move on and keep grindin'. Unfortunately for me, the negative belief system that I formed through my addictions took away any sense of self care and going to the gym became a distant memory. By losing the motivation to work out I diminished my overall health and opportunity for growth in the physical health department. A sedentary lifestyle does not lead to anything positive or successful, but rather to severe depression and a beer belly. Thankfully, that equal balance has reemerged in my life and I have taken my workouts to a whole new level. No longer am I that 236-pound imposter lying in a hospital bed. I am back to my typical healthy solid 205 and that makes looking in the mirror a whole lot easier.

When we exercise the brain releases chemicals called endorphins which help create a positive feeling within the body as well as reduce the feeling of pain. This is why exercising is one of the best-known ways to cope with stress. And who doesn't deal with stress at some point or another? Not only will exercising help create positive vibes on the inside, it also builds up our external figure. My brother likes to remind me of the acronym " LGFG: Look good, feel good" and I couldn't agree more with that statement. Whether we like it or not, the way we view how our body looks is a large contributing factor to our self-esteem. That useless scale might be packed away in the basement but avoiding mirrors for the rest of our lives is unnecessary. By working out a few times a week at your local health club, play tennis with a girlfriend on weekends, or walk your dog each morning while doubling up with the baby in the stroller, you will gain confidence about yourself inside and out. You can do it.

Less stress along with more smiling will defeat those negative thoughts and begin the process of loving yourself again.

They say you are what you eat, right? Who is this *they* that *they* speak of anyways? A healthy lifestyle is not just about hitting the gym to boost our self-esteem by building up our external appearance. If our diet is overloaded with fast-food, sweets, soda, and frozen dinners then we will feel the impact, literally. Our moods are directly affected by the food we consume. Foods that are rich in sugar cause our blood sugar levels to spike and once they drop back down that lethargic feeling kicks in.

As my friend and owner of *The Oakland Fitness Co.* in Oakland, CA Mike Beatrice puts it, "People need to start eating carbs again. People are lacking energy because of the lack of food intake or improper nutrient timing. Eating healthy tastes delicious. Healthy clean carbs, healthy fats, and lean protein as a base." We deplete our energy by what we eat. Laziness is not a positive characteristic, sorry to all the procrastinators out there. By eating healthy you will "never need to diet or deprive yourself of good food" which Beatrice says is done by creating balance in your nutritional approach. If you don't know how to cook, then watch some *Kitchen Nightmares* reruns and take notes from Gordon Ramsey in your new notebook. Not only does cooking make you an increasingly well-rounded individual, but it is a great way to impress a date. By learning healthier alternatives, you will create a healthier immune system. A healthier immune system means you are less likely to get sick and with "less sick days you get more days to hustle, more days to work, more days to exercise, more days to spend with loved ones, and more days to get money!" With that attitude it is no wonder Mike is a walking definition of success.

I am guilty as charged when it comes to my daily dose of a Dunk's iced coffee, but otherwise the only liquid going into my body is good ole H2O. If you are working out on a consistent basis then sweets on occasion are an earned treat for your hard work. That is the time to have a slice of ice cream cake at your son's birthday party, but please remember to leave some for his friends. Don't get too crazy as food comas should not be a part of your daily regime.

Our bodies are not designed to be filled with garbage that we know is unhealthy, yet we still intentional ingest. Tony Robbins conveys it perfectly in his national bestseller *Awaken the Giant Within*. He discusses our physical conditions importance as one of the five areas of life we need to work on mastering; "We cram our bodies with high-fat, nutritionally empty foods, poison our systems with cigarettes, alcohol, and drugs, and sit passively in front of our TV sets." Does that sound familiar? I can reluctantly say I unquestionably pass the 'sorry body, but I'm an addict' test, sans the cigarettes, an awfully negative habit I am happy to say I never once partook in. The finishing sentence from Robbins Physical Mastery portion says it best; "You not only look good, but you *feel* good and know that you're in *control* of your life, in a body that radiates vitality and allows you to accomplish outcomes." How true is that? Just think of the feeling you get after you eat fast food. It isn't pleasant.

"Confidence is contagious. So is lack of confidence."

- Vince Lombardi -

If being a positive person is what you seek, then you need to begin to spend your time around positive people. The old saying goes 'misery likes company' and that certainly is a miserable place to be. When you wake up I want you to tell yourself, "Today is going to be a great day!" while the miserable will be having a hissy fit about their day ahead. If you want to get things done, then make it a point to be around the people who get things done.

We know that there will always be those who doubt you, no matter what. Great, more motivation for you to succeed. Those who are constantly putting others down, dwelling on their own failures, and attempting to disrupt others' dreams are the ones we need to stay far away from and rid from our lives. While all of these poor souls complain about everything they can, you see the opportunity to find a solution to the problem. You have too much talent to let anyone drag you down. Stick with the winners and you will inherit the characteristics that they embody. Their positive outlook and attitudes on life will soon begin to wear off on you. You will see how they do not quit, they do not give up, they keep on keeping on, and follow through until completion. Successful people believe in whatever effort is necessary. They do not make excuses, and neither will you now that you're equipped with the necessary tools to break through the barriers on your way to the top.

When successful people themselves face an unexpected obstacle, they do not turn and run for the hills. And they certainly do not start playing the blame game. A successful person will assess the situation, figure out what needs to be fixed to move forward in a positive direction, and then respond accordingly with the necessary action. There is no mountain high enough to deter them from achieving their goals. Positive people also understand that there is no limit to what they can achieve, no dream too big, nor any vision too bold. Nothing will cut through their laser focus. These are the people you want to be surrounding yourself with, not the sorry saps who settle for less. We all need to focus on what we can do, not what we cannot. The possibilities are endless with a positive state of mind.

Remember that confidence you had when you were a kid thinking you could conquer anything in the world? Well, it's time to find that confidence again to build the belief that you can do it and you will get 'er done! If you aren't confident in yourself how can others be confident in you? The next time you walk into a room I can almost guarantee you will spot the confident person with a leadership mentality within minutes. That person will be you if you want it to be. My colleague Sarah Ordo goes into detail about the confidence factor in her second book *Innerbloom*. When speaking about confidence she states; "Can't you just tell when you see someone walking around with confidence? You can literally see it in the way they walk, the way they talk, and the way they act." The confident person is the one standing tall full of swagger and conversing with a smile on his or her face.

I have gotten the pleasure to know Sarah over the past few months while writing this book and her energy is nothing but radiant and positive. It is safe to say that Sarah is that person who others are surrounding themselves with these days, anxious to learn how her smile got so big. She is living proof that we can overcome any challenges that life may throw at us and is a true inspiration to myself. I read her first book, *Sober As F**ck during the beginning stages of my recovery in the detox facility I checked myself into. Her confidence, drive, and passion for living a life full of happiness, alcohol and drug free, oozed through the pages rubbing directly off on me.

One of the first major changes I felt take place within once I got back on my feet was regaining my confidence, my drive, and my passion for life that had been hidden away for many years, as it did for Sarah. Like Austin Powers, I call it my mojo and boy, was it back with a vengeance of which I owe a great deal of that to her. She tackled her addictions and coinciding depression head on and the word no was *no* longer in her vocabulary. She didn't make any excuses, she just produced results. This is the attitude and approach I have acquired in my journey of recovery versus the pundits and the negative people in my life who tell me I can't. Those people have been unfriended because I do not need anyone who is hindering me from achieving my goals and dreams. By dismissing those who are negatively affecting your life you have eliminated one more obstacle on your path to greatness. My vision is concise and unapologetic with all the pessimists quickly fading out of sight in the rearview mirror.

There is a reason the confident, the successful, and the winners always seem to be surrounded by crowds of people and that's because others want to have that swagger rub off on them. People want to learn the how and why of their confidence so they can look to regain their own. Who doesn't want to be surrounded by happy people who possess positive energy? We are well aware that there is no fun living in misery. Find that confident person the next time you are out at a gathering instead of standing solo in the corner waiting for someone to approach for you probably will be waiting a while. Be a participant not a bystander.

Not So Hans Solo

To achieve greatness, the ultimate success, the dreams you believed were just that, dreams, is not a solo mission. Everything you achieve in life comes from the help of others. Part of the process of picking yourself up when you are down is to remember that you are not alone, especially for those battling addiction. What you have been through someone else has, too. How you respond is what will determine where you go. The majority of people who have given up on life have an excuse for every hardship that has come about in their life. They have become a professional player in the blame game, never taking accountability for their actions nor circumstances. I am telling you there are no more excuses, there is only action to be taken from here on out. You have already begun the process by joining me on this march in reading *Stop Thinking Like That*. You are no longer alone. Start to use those that you wish to be like as inspiration and motivation to better your own life. And once you do, just keep grindin'.

A life in solitude leaves us extremely exposed to negativity. Living in what seemed like the never-ending Groundhog Day world of addiction held me back from any chance at personal growth. I was only hurting myself more with each step backwards and soon enough any hope of a better life for me had sunk down next to the Titanic. I had developed an exceedingly negative belief system and had no desire to put in the work because I felt I did not deserve any type of happiness. All my friends were in the midst of successful careers, buying houses, and starting families of their own while I had become BFFLs with my couch telling myself I was destined for the life I knew as a child.

The misfortunes of my life had left me all alone at the pity party, occupancy of one. I would be living vicariously through the television shows I was watching because I never imagined I could have any type of luxury nor regain any happiness in my life. I succumbed to the doom and gloom mentality and what I saw on television was only available in a far-off fantasy land. Well, you know what? I still haven't found that world and I no longer want to. I wouldn't trade the life I live today with any of those characters I was glued to watching day in and day out. I have found my calling, my passion, and now my desires are no longer implausible. Over time my belief system changed, and I took that monumental first step forward. I haven't stopped grindin' since, continuously disrupting the negative thoughts and beliefs that try to seep back into my mind with a healthy dose of "I can, I will!" I have managed to pick myself up off that Atlantic seabed and upon reaching the surface saw nothing but a vast ocean full of opportunity. Your turn!

One of the most impactful moments I've experienced on this journey was the day I realized it is okay that I do not have all the answers. Life is about learning and making ourselves a better person than we were yesterday. There is an infinite amount of knowledge for us to keep busy for an infinite amount of time. I strive to become a lifetime learner, so I dove head first into a pool full of wisdom. It was evident my addictive personality took over and my new addiction is to be learning *more*!

I surrounded myself with powerful books, writing down synopses after each chapter, studying them at every opportunity to build my mind into a brigade full of knowledge. I want you to make your brain your new hobby! In the first four months of my recovery alone I read twenty-seven books, all of which were focused on helping me improve my life by becoming the best version of myself possible. I could not get enough of what sticking my nose into these books was giving me in the endless possibilities. I reread some influential books from my past, such as the inspiring story of Chris Herren in *Basketball Junkie* to Norman Vincent Peale's famous *The Power of Positive Thinking*. Reading these again helped me reengage with all the types of positivity that I had possessed before I allowed my life to slowly crumble. My subconscious mind acted as if it didn't miss a beat recollecting all the goodies it had ingested in the years prior and soon it all clicked.

Through dedication and discipline, I have learned to turn nearly all negative situations right around, disregarding the difficulty of the challenges they may bring. I always knew I had that "it" factor to become successful, to be happy, and to inspire others. Presently that is exactly what I am doing as my confidence grows with each passing day. I no longer simply hope for the best, instead I *know* the best will materialize if I put maximum effort into the work. I will never stop grindin'.

[14]

All Day, Everyday

"There may be people who have more talent than you, but there's no excuse for someone to work harder than you."

- Derek Jeter -

Being an athlete my entire life it has been instilled in me that I must do whatever it takes to be better than the competition. From an early age my father would constantly remind me that there is always going to be someone better than me out there. He told me someone somewhere is progressively working harder than I am in efforts to beat me. Losing was not an option in my household so I had to take my training and my commitment to excellence to another level. I distinctly remember my father taking me behind the grocery store in the dead of winter to hit me "skimmas" and "high, high, high pop ups" as we were enclosed by what seemed like colossal-sized snow banks. What he really was hitting to me were ground balls and fly balls, but with his enigmatic twist on them. I was maybe eight or nine years old training like I had a MLB showcase coming up. I have been pursuing greatness since those days of throwing no-hitters and hitting game-winning homeruns at Harry Ball Field, the home of Beverly Little League. That pursuit continues on indefinitely because we can *always* improve in all areas of life. Practice does not make perfect, it makes improvement. You may have all the talent and motivation in the world, but to experience personal growth you must have discipline, which we will explore momentarily.

The God given talent you may possess can only take you so far. If you are the smartest person in the room then you are in the wrong room. No matter how smart or talented you believe you are there is always someone smarter and one upping you. Those are the ones you need to put in the extra work for if you wish to surpass them some day. If you want to be the best you have to beat the best and if you cannot beat them then you might as well join them up at the top. As esoteric of a thought as it may seem, you, yes YOU, can have everything you have ever envisioned. Get up off your old leather La-Z-Boy recliner and attack life with an attitude of "no matter what". Practice playing follow the leader and you will inevitably succeed. The people you see that lead and succeed in all aspects of life wake up every morning and put their socks on the same way you do; one foot at a time. You may have come from different places, but the common denominator to success is taking the first step on the path to your destiny.

Having the talent is a great start, but we always need to remind ourselves that there are many ingredients in the recipe for greatness. John C. Maxwell states in his book *The 21 Irrefutable Laws of Leadership*, "Talent alone is never enough. It must be bolstered by character if a person desires to go far." How do we develop character? You start by being honest with yourself. Remember from Chapter 10 we discussed the need to be impeccable with our word to develop integrity? The more candid we can be with ourselves the more we will begin to be honest with others. Those around us will be less reluctant to pass along their ideas and knowledge to us because they see we possess the key ingredient of integrity. Trust goes a long way when it is formed in a relationship. The leaders you look up to will see your character being created through your honest personality allowing you to gain ground on learning what they know. Why? Because true leaders are willing to share their experiences with others especially with those that have earned their trust.

Building character also requires you to develop self-discipline. The renowned personal development coach Brian Tracy wrote a book on this topic called *The Miracle of Self-Discipline*. In his book he uses a quote from the 1800's American author and philosopher Elbert Hubbard who defines self-discipline as "The ability to make yourself do what you should when you should do it whether you feel like it or not." All too often we make excuses for why things are not getting done in our daily duties. We become expert procrastinators using the phrase "I will get to it later" on a daily basis. Well, what if the later never happens? Then what? This is why the *later* is NOW! If you want to experience growth in your life, then prepare yourself to begin taking massive action today and drop all your excuses off at the "unimprovement" office. Those who consistently achieve their goals are disciplined in taking the necessary action to get better every day. It doesn't matter how big or small the action you have enhanced yourself in, the fact that you improved is progression. For me, I know once my head hits the pillow at night and I haven't had a drink or a drug in that day then I had myself an extremely productive day. The grind never stops for us when we relentlessly chase down our dreams.

Andrew Carnegie to Richard Branson and every successful person in between has developed daily positive habits by becoming a master in the art of self-discipline. Get up every morning with an attitude of gratitude, starting your day off on a positive note, then work your tail off all day and you will see yourself begin to develop those attractive habits. Do you want to become part of the elite 1% of Americans who own much of our country's wealth? Be the first one to arrive at the office and the one turning the lights off at the end of the day. Be the ball player who is taking those extra hacks off a tee after every practice or shooting a couple hundred free throws while your teammates are on their way home checking their Facebooks. Read, read, and read some more, expanding your knowledge in whatever aspiration you're seeking. Do not ever settle! If you want it bad enough you will commit yourself to the process and that requires a mastery of self-discipline.

Today, right now, I want you to start practicing daily discipline by unearthing a new positive habit that will build growth within and help you inch closer to your ultimate destination. Upon waking up, before you head out for your day, is when this habit will become part of your daily morning routine. Continue practicing this habit every morning for a week straight. Notice the differences in your days, particularly the increase in your awareness and mindfulness of the environment around you. Don't stop for the rest of the month allowing this one positive habit to take its place in your life. Go ahead and write down your new positive habit below. It all starts NOW!

My exciting new daily positive habit is: ____________________

____

____

____

____

In order for you to start experiencing growth in your personal development you must practice self-discipline every day Monday through Sunday. There are "NO DAYS OFF!" If you don't believe me please go ask what many say is the greatest coach of all time, Bill Belichick. He famously chanted the phrase "No days off!" during one of his New England Patriots Super Bowl Champion parades. Since Belichick became the head coach of the Patriots in 2000 they have won so many Lombardi's it is easy to mix up all the parades. The Patriots dynasty of the 2000's to current are a model of consistency showing the world what you can accomplish when you devote yourself to the practice of self-discipline and the greatness that can come together by putting trust in the others beside you on your journey.

Discipline is one of the fifteen ways to maximize your potential in Maxwell's *How Successful People Grow.* He defines discipline as "the bridge between goals and accomplishments, and that bridge must be crossed every day." Discipline is an everyday matter of constant improvement. Once discipline is instilled in us we begin traveling on the road to greatness.

Cal Ripken Jr. did not become one of the greatest shortstops to ever lace 'em up by being content and complacent. His daily routine of discipline and consistency allowed him to play in 2,632 straight games for the Baltimore Orioles, never missing a single game over a sixteen-year span. Think about that for a minute? Imagine going to work every single day for sixteen straight years? It was an incredible milestone and may be the most unsurpassable feats in all of sports. Ripken is the ultimate example of self-discipline, working hard every single day to expand his game in any one of the five-tools baseball players are rated on, and of putting in the necessary work vying for improvement. I am not asking you to go work every day for the next sixteen years, as I want you to be able to reap the benefits of your hard work at times, as well. However, the message is clear; if you want to be the best at what you do then you must be willing to do whatever it takes. You must be disciplined. You must never stop grindin'.

[15]

Quit Playing Games with Your Heart

"Being deeply loved by someone gives you strength, while loving someone deeply gives you courage."

- Lao Tzu -

What is love? Everyone yearns to be loved, but what does that really mean? How would you define it? Brené Brown digs deep into love in her book *Gifts of Imperfection.* She is spot on with her thoughts on what love is when she says; "We cultivate love when we allow our most vulnerable and powerful selves to be deeply seen and known, and when we honor the spiritual connection that grows from that offering with trust, respect kindness, and affection." As discussed previously, when we allow ourselves to be vulnerable we open our hearts up for better or worse. Brown doesn't feel love is something we hand out or are given, stating "we neither give nor receive it; it's something we nurture and grow, a connection that can only be cultivated." Love is the most human feeling one can experience. Yes, it is an experience to me, as I believe love is an action word! The gift of love brings a sense of peace and true joy to one's life. You can say "I love you!" all you want, but it is felt by the actions you take.

I can do nothing but smile right now as my mind wanders off to the feeling of sharing love with another person. I would like to think I have experienced true love in my life whether it be with a significant other or genuine love from/for a friend. Family love is always a touchy subject during our most challenging times especially if they're self-induced problems, but even if it is tough love, it shows you that you have people in your life that care about you. You have people that love you. You are never alone.

Broken hearts regularly became part of my repertoire, something that I am not proud of, but you live and learn. Families, friends, and loved ones are dragged through the mud by the alcoholics and addicts. The old saying goes that alcoholics lie, cheat, and steal and there is nothing different in my story. My addictions to *more* completely stripped me of all my ethical values, morals and spiritual being. I became an expert manipulator to anyone close to me so much so that I didn't even realize I was doing it. I would say whatever you wanted to hear in order for me to get what I wanted. I was a chameleon at his finest. The smart girlfriend would catch on and run for the hills without a trace trying not to lose any more time in her life with a dirty rotten scoundrel like myself. It didn't last much longer for the poor souls who stayed before I got bored and yet again, more hearts were broken. I can say these things about myself without batting an eye because I have accepted and owned up to my actions knowing they will never ever happen again as long as I stay sober. We all have our flaws, but they only define us if we allow them to.

Not to toot my own horn, but I think sober me is a pretty awesome guy. Sober me shows love, he doesn't just announce it to appease the situation or his loved one's mind. I have always said that I'm a hopeless romantic and I stand by that to this day. The unconditional love from my mother made me cherish the feelings of love and affection that a relationship would bring. If I could make you happy and put a smile on your face then I would go to great lengths to do so. I have often been told my heart is too big and I can care too much to a fault. This all makes perfect sense growing up as the only child of a hardworking single mom. I was constantly pushing to help others any chance I could get because I saw how hard she worked to make sure I was taken care of. But give me a couple shots followed by any number of drugs and you no longer existed in Jason's world for that world was a party of one.

Even though, for the addict, we are hurting ourselves more than anyone, the people who love and care about us are being endlessly dragged in the mud by our actions. No one should ever feel less than, but don't tell us that. The lack of respect and loyalty sickens me even thinking about it. If you are reading this and I have hurt you in the past please know that "I am truly sorry and I never intentionally meant any harm. I understand if you do not forgive me."

All we can do is learn from the mistakes, regrets and the shameful acts from our past to make sure they will never happen again. Don't forget pain and suffering are part of the process in learning to love ourselves once again as well as in developing the best possible version of ourselves we can be. No words can take back the hurt and pain we have caused to many people along our paths of destruction. I will never use drugs and or alcohol as an excuse for any of my past actions or transgressions, but anyone who knows me understands I was a completely different person when substances were involved.

Needless to say, I certainly am well versed on what not to do in a relationship, romantic or platonic. However, go reread the "Public Service Announcement" and follow it rigorously. Yes, I did have many loving enjoyable times in each relationship I have been a part of but also brought to light in each were my character defects and that is where the learning process begins.

We need to learn from our flaws for, again, they do not define us. What is done is done and it will never come back. It is time to find out who we really are capable of being so let go of who you *were* because that person is a thing of the past. You are a loving caring person and the first person I need you to work on loving is YOURSELF. After finding the love for yourself you can begin to spread all the love and joy to those around you. To me there is not a better feeling in the world than experiencing love and YOU deserve to feel that, too. Now please smile for me for this is just the beginning of a beautiful life ahead for you.

Perfect Happiness

No one is perfect. Period. I have made it very clear we all have flaws and that's part of what makes us human. We can chase perfection until the cows come out, but like a puppy trying to catch his own tail, you'll be forever running in circles.

As a former professional athlete, I am all too familiar with always being pushed to be perfect. We are constantly being told how to satisfy other's needs, very rarely our own. Apparently, we are supposed to chase something that is as rare as lochness monster sightings. In the over 140 years of Major League Baseball there have only been 23 perfect games ever thrown. A perfect season in the

80+ years of the NFL? Achieved once by the '72 Dolphins. Damn you David Tyree!

The old saying of "practice makes perfect" needs to be adjusted to "practice makes improvement". We can strive for excellence, but we will never achieve perfection. The chase will last a lifetime if we do. There is *always* room for improvement and that is what we should be motivated to do on a daily basis. I had a sign painted on a wall at my fitness facility that was the mantra for AP+ that said #getbettereveryday. If you are better today than you were yesterday than that is progress in the right direction! Success is growth every day.

Expecting perfection is NOT something only athletes live with. Everyone is pushed at some level in their life to a certain degree, but it is how we react to the shoves that of concern. Unfortunately, it is a never-ending story hearing about people losing their way in life because they simply cannot live up to another's expectations. Always remind yourself that you do not need to be perfect to be happy for perfection does not exist. Stick with moving forward and doing the next right thing and happiness will undoubtedly follow. True happiness begins with being happy with who we are as individuals. When that occurs, we can then share the joy in life with everyone around us from our loved ones to the strangers we pass walking down the street.

Dale Carnegie published one of the more prominent books of its kind in *How To Make Friends and Influence People* back in 1936. Its principles are still very relevant in society today. A very quick read, but filled with extremely impactful content, from the start he goes through "Six Ways to Make People Like You" of which the second rule is simply to *smile.* Carnegie describes a letter he received from a New York stockbroker by the name of William B. Steinhardt. The author of the letter is a student in one of Carnegie's classes in which the group is given the assignment to smile every hour of the day at someone for an entire week.

Steinhardt describes himself as a grouchy old man, married for eighteen plus years, and rarely if ever smiles. He went on to practice the art of smiling every morning for two months straight and the results were astonishing. He said, "This changed attitude of mine has brought more happiness in our home during these two months than there was during the last year. As I leave for my office now, I greet the elevator boy in the apartment house with a 'Good morning' and a smile. I greet the doorman with a smile. I smile at the cashier in the subway booth when I ask for change. As I stand on the floor in the Curb Exchange, I smile at men who never saw me smile until recently. I soon found that everyone was smiling back at me." It is amazing how far a simple smile can go, isn't it? Steinhardt further stated he "eliminated criticism from my system. I give appreciation and praise now instead of condemnation. I have stopped talking about what I want. I am now trying to see the other person's viewpoint. And these things have literally revolutionized my life. I am a totally different man, a **happier** man, a richer man, richer in friendships and happiness -- the only things that matter after all."

As we discussed during the chapter on positive thinking, smiling has been scientifically proven to provide us with happiness. How so you ask? We use certain muscles to produce a smile that trigger the brain to sense happiness when these muscles are activated. The same can be said with the muscles we use when we frown triggering our brain to think something must be wrong. Smiles are infectious and often they will make those you smile at give you a glowing smile right back. From there? You guessed it. Their brain is now sensing happy times ahead from the mere fact that you gave them a friendly hello smile. You never know how much these unpretentious smiles you give complete strangers may mean to them.

The story Carnegie shares with his readers provides evidence that smiling can lead to a richer life, both literally and figuratively, not only for yourself, but for those who you share your smiles with. Smiling enriches our day and the days of those around us. Someone could be having the worst day of their life and your smile just gave them that little hope they needed that everything is going to be okay. Therefore, do not forget Rule #2 to making people like you, and SMILE ... for life is good! Say "CHEESE!"

I like to think that we all deserve happiness in our lives. Deserving as we may be, though, happiness is still an emotion we must earn. How do we earn it? We need to find out for ourselves from the inside without reliance from outside circumstances. Happiness derives from within. If the grouchy stockbroker can find joy in life so can YOU. The first step he took in seeking out this newfound emotion was taking the action to change. He was willing to make an attitude adjustment knowing that was the only way for things to truly change for him. With his open mind and willingness to change he soon found out the effect a positive attitude and a smile had not only on himself but also to those around him. Steinhardt was able to share his joy and happiness with others and this revolutionized his life. Spreading these blissful sensations brings a *permagrin* to my face and I don't doubt it will do the same for you. You need to be open and willing and endless opportunities of good things await.

As I walk up to the plate I feel like I've been here before. I feel as if this isn't new to me, yet the scene is different now. All my teammates are younger than I, but nonetheless I know the outcome before I even see my first pitch. I'm trotting around the bases amidst the roar of my teammates exploding from the dugout. The National Championship game is now all knotted at four. Everything else about the dream is so vivid and real, from the giant Kudzo Hill behind right field to the tears streaming down my face due to defeat. Yes, I did hit a homerun to tie the National Championship game at four, but that was all the scoring we could muster up leading to a second-place finish. After watching the Mules pig pile on the infield grass following the final out, my name rang loudly over the stadium's public announcement system; "The 2003 Division II College World Series Most Outstanding Player, Jay Hyland!" It wasn't the accomplishment I sought out as we entered Montgomery, but it was a proud accomplishment nonetheless. Especially coming from the losing team. Bitter-Sweet Home Alabama.

I wake up to my alarm clock radio blaring "Hotstepper" in a state of confusion. In reality, the team in the opposing dugout wasn't Kansas City, it was Central Missouri State. Either way they were from the same state and went on to take the Title over us 11-4.

I love when I dream about baseball, especially these days when it seems like every other night I am dreaming about exes, booze, or drugs. The trifecta of my destruction. One of the many blessings of sobriety is all the messes that you thought you had suppressed away for good start reemerging into your mind. Insert sarcasm here. I've been told to become acquainted with these occurrences the longer I am abstinent from drugs and alcohol. Oh joy! Insert sarcasm here.

---

[16]

Courage Under Fire

"He who is not courageous enough to take risks will accomplish nothing in life."

- Muhammad Ali -

Are you Mike Tyson or Buster Douglas? Tyson is in the conversation of the greatest heavyweight boxer of all time, but clearly was complacent and thought he could get by on his natural ability the night of the fight. Douglas proved that you always have a fighter's chance no matter the opposition you are facing. His knockout of Tyson is the ultimate underdog story. The courage that

David showed to even go up against Goliath was inconceivable. He was undeterred in his quest to prove everyone wrong especially his father and brothers. Like we discussed prior, adversity comes in many forms including from our own disbelieving families. If you have the courage of a Buster Douglas or a David to stand up and go after what you want and attack your fears then you are already ahead of the game.

Everyone possesses courage inside themselves but not all seek to find it. When you do then you are telling yourself everything is going to be alright and it is okay to just be YOU and not who others want you to be. Are there any movies that you simply cannot get through without your face getting a little puffy and your eyes filling up with water? It's okay, I do as well, so we can stop blaming it on something prancing around in our eye. There are two such movies for me that turn into incredibly motivating tearjerkers. My childhood favorite *E.T.* aside, *The Pursuit of Happyness* and *The Blind Side* have that effect on me. Both films are based around courageous characters who overcome massive odds against them to live a rewarding life.

The main characters of the two films exemplify courage and are living proof that *anything* is possible. Let's start with the character Will Smith plays in *The Pursuit of Happyness*, Christopher Gardner. Chris is a tremendously hardworking single father who ends up at one point with the unfortunate scenario of living in a subway bathroom...with his son. Yes, there were misfortunate events that occurred to him impacting not only his life, but his son's as well. Did he blame the mother of his child, the economy, the jerk at the motel who kicked him out, or the fact that he was African-American as the reason for his demise? Absolutely not! Life happens and how we respond to its events determines where we go. No matter the circumstances Gardner was not going to be denied in providing the life that he wanted for his son. Whatever it took, he was willing to do it. Gardner just kept grindin'.

While walking around San Francisco selling the infamous now defunct bone density scanner to any doctor that would listen, he somehow was managing to also fight as one of twenty interns for the one spot a large brokerage firm in the city was looking to fill. Despite having to work (unpaid) less hours than the other nineteen candidates Chris found a way to rise above the rest of the pack by honing his craft of contacting potential clients for the firm.

In the initial meeting with all the company's top brass in a boardroom Gardner arrives not in a presentable suit, but with paint all over himself. The night prior he was painting the walls of his own apartment for his landlord to help cut down his rent when San Francisco's finest came knocking and took him down to the station for unpaid *parking* tickets. From there, covered in paint, he ran to the office building and into that boardroom in a paint stained shirt. Whatever it takes. The Cinderella story culminates with Chris earning that coveted position and ultimately, he continues his path to even greater heights by starting his own multi-million-dollar firm.

The waterfalls on my face emerge when on the last day of the internship the firm gives Gardner the exciting news; "Wear one tomorrow though, okay? Because tomorrow's going to be your first day." referencing their last meeting when Gardner arrived in the t-shirt splattered in paint. Yes, I couldn't help but to pause my writing and go to You-Tube to watch this scene, immediately causing goose bumps and chills to cover my entire body. An elated Gardner walks out into the hustle and bustle of the San Francisco streets clapping his hands with tears running down his face as a Will Smith voice-over says, "This part of my life, this part right here is what I call *happyness.*"

Chris Gardner is the epitome of a "whatever it takes" attitude. After seeing the movie for the first time (dozens since) I told myself that if Gardner can do it, why can't I? I had no more excuses as to why I couldn't achieve greatness, as to why I couldn't reach a point in my life I could call true *happyness* myself. Like we have discussed all along, but in a direct manner: If you want it you can have it, but you must work for it. Chris Gardner personifies all the things we have discussed throughout *Stop Thinking Like That* that are necessary to get through the tough times, to pick ourselves off the ground, to experience success, to reach out and grab a hold of greatness, and to live a fulfilling happy life.

It is pretty evident that athletics have played a significant role in my life, from my earliest memories of child hood right up to this bitter cold December day. Athletics certainly have helped form the person that I am today, most notably the leadership characteristics I believe I possess, the confidence factor, and the literal "hate to lose" mentality. The great thing about sports is you can relate them to nearly all the challenges we face in life, the day to day grind, and the joy success brings us. I have used plenty analogies proving this is the case, but the following story is the decisive resource for proof that athletics can help us get through any challenge that may confront us and Michael Oher is that proof. More so, this individual proves that no matter what the circumstances, no matter the odds that are stacked up against you, you CAN overcome anything!

Michael Oher is the subject of the movie *The Blind Side*. Played by Quinton Aaron, Oher is an inner city African-American living amidst the everyday abuse of alcohol, addiction, violence, alongside his crack-cocaine addicted mother with no father in sight. It is an unfortunate, but all-too familiar story that many of today's youth face in our inner-city communities. It is not uncommon for these said youth to end up following the cycle of joining gangs, abusing drugs, being absentee parents, abusing their families, and regrettably abusing themselves to the point of living short, destructive lives. It's not uncommon for children growing up under these circumstances to get caught up in the trap and continue the trend. This is the easy way out for them, a simple cop out blaming they're a product of their environment.

You have a better chance to find a four-leaf clover than to find a young child who doesn't conceivably accept living in constant fear, poverty, and experiencing or witnessing abuse, bucking the trend. However, Michael Oher is that four-leaf clover. His courageous efforts brought to light to an entire nation the endless possibilities life has for us if we are willing and open. By all means he was dealt an iniquitous hand in life. While living in foster care, Michael runs away and finds himself sleeping on a friend's couch. The friend's father began the implausible journey for Oher. The loquacious man talks his way into having both his child and his son's friend, Michael, get admitted into a perennial white Christian high-school. Did I mention Oher stands 6'4" and weighs over 300 pounds? The coach of the school's football program, the now former University of Mississippi head coach Hugh Freeze, had both the friend and Oher enrolled per certain academic obligations being satisfied. Befriended by a younger student, Oher eventually is adopted by the boy's family, the Tuohys, who are an extremely prominent family within the community, and unaccustomed wealth soon filled Michael's world. While living with them, Mrs. Tuohy, played by Sandra Bullock, offers Michael a guest room with a bed, in which he responds with "I've never had one before." She assumes he is speaking about having his own room, but he brings tears to her and my eyes (and probably to audiences all over) when he corrects her by stating "A bed."

Michael Oher ends up becoming an All-American lineman at the University of Mississippi and is drafted in the first round of the 2008 NFL draft by the Baltimore Ravens. He goes from being passed around foster homes in inner city Memphis to becoming an instant millionaire in the NFL. His success was by no means instant and it is certainly not about the money, but rather the rocky journey that brought him the success and wealth. The courage it took Oher to get to where he is today is astonishing, if not miraculous. With little discipline nor education and surrounded by drugs and violence, he chose to say YES to attending what must have seemed like another planet in a predominantly white Christian high school. He then chose to work tirelessly to not only hone his craft as a football player, a sport he never played prior to high school, but more importantly in the classroom.

Michael did not make *any* excuses for the circumstances life presented to him as a youth, instead he chose to use those experiences as motivation for a better life for himself. Even more so, Oher provides hope and faith to anyone who is struggling in life with poverty, abuse, addiction, violence, and many other unforeseen exogenous factors. His courageous actions transcended more than the game of football, they gave hope for a better life to anyone living in deplorable conditions. He did not merely show the inner-city youth of America what is possible when we take courageous actions to take a step forward into the unknown. He showed us all.

Nearly all of society has lived through traumatic experiences that we wish we could expel from our mind. It is not the experience itself that determines the path we take, but the response we create to handling said adversity. You must push through these debilitating times no matter how difficult and unimaginable it may seem. There is no time to remain stagnant for the further we fall victim to a morose being, the deeper the hole we are digging ourselves. I can tell you firsthand please avoid doing this at ALL costs. Life is not easy as it is, I get that, but we don't need to add any unnecessary issues on ourselves by playing the poor-me card.

I highly suggest if you have not done so already, to dig out your Blockbuster card and rent *The Pursuit of Happyness* and *The Blind Side.* Seriously though, search for these movies online, on DVD, or on-demand somewhere, grab a bag of popcorn and some Kleenex, and watch the power of courage unfold. You will witness all types of stereotypes and stigmas get stomped down like the obstacles life inevitably present you. If you want it, there is no excuse that you cannot have it. I won't hear it! If you find yourself dishing out blame and making excuses, quickly recall the exorbitant odds that Christopher Gardner and Michael Oher overcame on their unexpected road to happiness and success. There are no more excuses, you have dominion over them from here on out! Just keep grindin'!

[17]

Conclusion

"VICTORY!"

- Johnny Drama *Entourage* -

Did you make it out alive? That wasn't so hard after all, was it? We are a society who always seem to make mountains out of mole hills; a characteristic of negative thinking. With a negative mind, catastrophic thinking takes over with the anticipation of the worst-case scenario as the only outcome we allow our brains to conceive. This is no longer how your brain works, for positivity is running rampant within. Your focus is now on the abundance in life that you already hold rather than what which you are lacking.

Digging through all the bullshit of our past hurts, and we probably went through a box or two of tissues in doing so. But, your past is no longer going to consume your mind anymore. Hope and positivity are the new residents within your brain. With faith and a positive mindset, achieving the life you have always thought was only found on Netflix and in Red Boxes will no longer seem too distant. Your reality is your choice. Choose wisely.

The journey of life is something that will challenge you, me, and the rest of the population for the remainder of our days on this beautiful earth. There are no secrets or shortcuts to overcoming life's tragic events, finding real happiness, or experiencing greatness. The answers to *how it works* lie within these pages. However, I could tell you until I am blue in the face what is necessary to unearthing the greatest version of yourself that exists. But only you can put in ALL the work required and commit to constantly taking massive action. One of my mom's favorite phrases sums it up; "You can lead a horse to water, but you cannot make it drink."

No matter the struggles you may be facing right now they will pass. Life will go on. Of course, I know many of us are living each day filled with an inordinate amount of emotional damage. That, too, will pass. The failures and adversity will never stop. All that means is neither will the opportunities to learn more and experience growth. See that right there? How I turned a negative into a positive? There is one of the first keys to getting yourself off that musty, basement sofa and up opening the shades. You can find the good and positive in every situation that arrives at your feet. It is up to you to make it happen.

As for the critics trying to hold you down? How dare someone have the audacity to put a cap on YOUR potential. You are the only person at fault when you walk away from your dreams because of the ignorance of another human being. You are better than that! The talent within you is ready to burst at the seams as it anxiously awaits the removal of the mask the real you has been hiding behind. Once the cover is removed you will feel a tremendous sense of relief with freedom now at your beck and call.

Personally, the day I removed the mask that revealed the scared, hopeless, depressed, shameful individual that I believed I had become was the very day of my rebirth. If you recall during the beginning of this journey, I stated there was a day that I deemed "the first day of the rest of my life". Well, that was the day I ripped off the mask that had been suppressing growth for me for years. There was no more need to rehearse and memorize the trail of lies that consumed my days while keeping my addictions a deep dark secret. The relief of not having to chase down the origin of an initial lie was exhilarating and refreshing at the same time. I now had all this newfound energy and time that were being robbed from me by my dishonesty.

The cap that I had seemingly applied to my life and sealed shut flew off and a flurry of potential was unleashed. Along with it came self-love, confidence, ambition, and most importantly, self-worth. There is no longer a cap, whether his, hers, or theirs, that can inhibit me from achieving all that I inspire and desire to have. This is what awaits you once you no longer accept a life lived with limitations and restrictions, whether set by society or self-induced. As *Scarface* reminds us, "The world is yours!", just don't go becoming an international drug kingpin. RIP Tony Montana.

Never forget that you have a defining purpose and that greatness lies within every one of you. Lindsey Cartwright is the CEO of L.C. Events, a company she founded after ten years working within the field of event coordinating and planning. With her firsthand experience of the industry she was ready to take on a bigger role and entrepreneurship was calling her name.

I spoke with Lindsey, whom I have gotten the pleasure to know in the past few months while writing *Stop Thinking Like That* through our passion for athletics, about how she deals with the struggles that come along with being an independent woman entrepreneur striving for a life second to none. She exclaimed, "I've had to deal with many hardships...and have had many excuses to just give up, but I won't. I keep on moving forward because it's going to make one hell of a story when I make it!" That statement reiterates what we have been deliberating all throughout *Stop Thinking Like That*; we all will experience hardships in our lives and those times seem to always fall onto our laps at the worst times possible. The question is, are you going to join Lindsey, myself, and the countless others who are living fulfilling lives, and bulldoze your way through life's obstacle course? Or are you going to continue sulking on your mother's couch watching endless amounts of reality television?

The show ever present during my self-victimization was *American Pickers.* Mike and Frank were thankfully always there for me during the most depressing times I have experienced in my life. They became part of the Hyland family; Beanie, Shaq, the Pickers, and me enjoying the doom and gloom existence together. One of the many joys of being in active addiction (sarcasm). I never did thank them nor apologize for my sudden departure. Sorry guys! It is never too late to do anything that your splendid mind desires including saying goodbye to reality TV and the desolate life that accompanies it.

"Two roads diverged in a wood, and I —

I took the one less traveled by,

And that has made all the difference."

-Robert Frost *The Road Not Taken*-

So, here you are standing at the bottom of an unfamiliar staircase, staring up to what seems like eternity. Then to your right you have a fully-functioning elevator. You have two choices at this moment;

take the quick and easy route of stepping into that elevator and proceeding to hit the button to the penthouse. Or are you willing to take the challenge of walking up those stairs one step at a time to see what you're made of? There is no elevator you can hop on to get through life unscathed. There is no button to press that takes you directly to the top, only the challenges that those stairs present will get you there. Continue taking the elevator and you'll continue living in a life of monotony, going with the flow of each passing day, with no direction or ambition.

Envision yourself climbing one stair at a time, pushing through the pain, wiping away the sweat pouring down your face, and confronting every controversial step along the way head on. The staircase of life is full of adversity to test your will, but you have got to keep grindin'. When you find yourself at a standstill staring at a creaky, unstable stair, pause, assess the situation and trust that you will be okay by proceeding forward. A leg might slip through, but no obstacle is fierce enough to halt your climb to the top. No cuts or bruises are going to stop you. Attack those stairs with an unstoppable determined mentality and you will conquer them, no matter how long it may take.

Be proud of yourself that you are no longer taking the lazy route through life by using the elevator. Be proud of the moment when you arrive at the peak. You deserve it. Once you catch your breath at the summit of this seemingly endless staircase, picking your hands up off your knees, and lifting your head high, you will see another flight of stairs, inexplicably higher than the last. You know what to do. Now go do it!

The past seven months I have endured an inordinate amount of emotions as my life has been one incredible and truly unbelievable roller coaster of a ride. The long winding road to happiness is one that I will be traveling for the rest of my life. Like with greatness, the chase for me has only begun. Am I happy today? Is that a trick question? I can honestly say that I have never felt more in touch with who I am, the person I was meant to be, than I am today. And that person is happy beyond belief. The feeling of purpose that has engulfed me is something that I cannot put into words (except in these 50,000 or so). I am already feeling anxious yet ecstatic for the inevitable day when you contact me to passionately exclaim that moment has occurred for you! I will be forever in the process of finding myself in the ever-changing world around me. As for now, I am simply following the overwhelming feeling deep in my gut that is constantly telling me "You can. You will. Just keep grindin'."

The End

Made in the USA
Columbia, SC
02 May 2018